Cashing In
On Free State Government Money

CASHING IN ON FREE STATE GOVERNMENT MONEY

By David Bendah

Some of the methods presented in this book may be illegal in certain parts of the United States. This book is sold for informational purposes only.

Library of Congress Cataloging in Publication Data
Bendah, David.
Cashing In On Free State Government Money.
   1. Small Business--United States--Finance--Directories.
   2. Government Lending--United States--Directories.
   I. Title.
HG4027.7.B473   1990   658.15'244--dc20   89-13690
ISBN 0-933301-02-2   CIP

Cashing In On Free State Government Money

Editorial and Desktop Assistance: David Brauner

Chapter One

State Help For Your Business

In addition to all the help the federal government provides to small businesses, the individual states also provide a wealth of assistance to small business owners who are in need. Realizing that the overall health of their economy depends on the prosperity of individual business owners, state governments make a special effort to encourage individual enterprise. If you need help starting or expanding your business, your state department of commerce is a good place to start. You will find the programs currently available listed here by state. Each has developed its own set of programs and aid packages specifically designed to help business hopefuls.

The types of assistance include: Free money in the form of grants, loans, loan guarantees, interest subsidies on loans, marketing help, business consulting and analysis, information regarding tax breaks and other financial incentives for businesses, employee training subsidies, management training, one-stop licensing and permit agencies, educational programs and research assistance. In addition, offices are set up in each state to help local businesses secure state and federal government contracts, and overseas business.

The second part of this book includes a brief mention of federal help available to small businesses through the Small Business Administration (SBA) and other related agencies: **Small Business Investment Companies (SBIC's), The Certified Development Corporation, Minority Small Business Enterprise Investment Companies (MESBIC's) and Minority Business Development Agencies.** Also included is a section on doing business with the federal government. This book on state help for businesses, together with our *How To Get Free Grants From The U.S. Government* - which lists the free money available from the federal government for mostly non-business needs like education, general welfare, housing, research and the arts - provide a comprehensive survey of government help. Private foundation grants for both individual and business-related needs are listed by state in another book, *The Secrets Of Getting Free Money*.

The National Governor's Association(NGA) is another fine place to seek help. It was organized to promote the interests of the individual states and territories of the United States and is an excellent source of information about state assistance programs for small businesses. In addition to providing details of specific programs already established in each state, staff at the NGA also can direct you to specific state agencies, associations and other organizations. Contact: **National Governor's Association, Hall of State, 444 North Capitol Street NW, Washington, DC 20009. (202) 624-5300.**

The Types Of Help Available

The next few pages are a summary of the type of help available, followed by a state-by-state rundown of the specific programs and agencies that exist in each state. The types of programs and assistance available depends upon the state; not every program is available in every state. For more information, contact the local state agencies listed here.

Funding

Free Money: Usually in the form of grants, this is money you don't have to pay back. As you might expect, free money is somewhat limited, but is available for those concerns and areas targeted for special attention. One such example is a Community Development Block Grant. Most states have some such program under which funds are provided to individuals, agencies or businesses intending on developing targeted areas, creating jobs, or in some way fulfilling a need or requirement designated by states as being important.

Loans: Like the federal government, states will lend business owners money directly, and usually at interest rates that are below market. States also set aside loan programs for those who have been turned down by commercial lenders. (These are similar to what is offered by the SBA.)

Loan Guarantees: These are loans obtained through commercial lenders which the state backs up. The SBA also provides this form of assistance designed to help business people obtain startup or expansion capital. Institutions are much more willing to lend to individuals who have the backing of the state. If such an individual defaults, the state is responsible for repaying the loans, so there is little risk to the lender.

Interest Subsidies: Under this program, the state will subsidize the interest rate charged by the bank on a loan. If you have a $100,000 loan at 10 percent interest, your payment - principal and interest - would be around $10,000 a year. Of this cost, the state might pay half of that $10,000, effectively cutting your interest rate in half.

Other Low-Interest Loans: There are other loans which the state provides at interest rates below market. Some of these are financed through the sale of general obligation bonds to the public. The public, of course, receives interest on the bonds they buy but at a slightly lower rate than is available from certificates of deposit and other high yield, low risk investments. To compensate, the buyers of these bonds receive a break on their taxes. Because investors receive less interest, those borrowing the funds pay less interest on the money borrowed. These loans usually are restricted to the purchase of fixed assets like equipment or a factory.

Venture-Capital Financing: In addition to the many thousands of private venture capital firms throughout the country, various states also are getting into the business. Venture capital is money that does not have to be paid back. In return for the funds they lend, venture capital firms take a slice of the business doing the borrowing. This "equity" is usually in the form of stocks or a percentage of future profits. Venture capitalists gamble that the firms they loan to will prosper and increase in value. States now can offer certain firms a chance to borrow under the same conditions. This method is commonly used by proven firms that need expansion money.

Employee-Training Funds: Many states have programs which disperse federal funds earmarked for the training of employees. Under this program, the state will pay part of an employee's salary while they are learning a job or acquiring a skill. This encourages the development of unskilled workers and increases the "marketability" of the work force. Other programs pay for the schooling and other educational advancement of employees.

Services and Equipment: Besides outright funding, states can also provide free or low-cost services and equipment. Such help includes office space, office equipment, telephone services, consulting and financial planning.

Tax Help: Many states offer reduced income tax liability to certain kinds of businesses or those located in targeted areas - often referred to as *Enterprise Zones.* Which businesses qualify depends on the needs of the state and the areas of commerce they wish to develop. Many states offer tax incentives as a way of attracting out of state businesses as well.

Consulting and Advice

Business Consulting: In addition to all the federal help offered through the SBA, states also provide free- and low-cost advice in the form of workshops, seminars and even one-on-one counseling for business people. Management training is also available. States are well aware that the lack of management expertise is one of the biggest causes of business failure. (The other is a lack of capital.)

Business Site Selection: Consulting is also available in this area. The state will provide expert advice to business owners trying to determine the best place to set up shop. The size of the available labor force is one key factor to be considered.

Market Studies: Many states will provide you with free or inexpensive marketing information. Each state collects demographic information concerning marketing within its borders and has access to those prepared by the federal government regarding national, and international data.

Research And Development: This help pertains to businesses that need specialized consulting help. Under this program, states put business owners in contact with professors and other experts from the academic world who are willing to share their expertise. A retail business needing help defining its market may seek the help of the Marketing Department of a university, for instance, or the Computer Engineering Department may be able to provide some assistance to a fledging computer software company.

Cutting Through the Red Tape: Many states have toll-free numbers set up to inform business owners about federal, state and local requirements, and how to "get legal." Some areas include licensing, regulations and permits.

Help In Getting Funds, Contracts and Business

Government Contracts: Special state offices have been established to help small businesses get lucrative government contracts. This includes local, state and federal help. If you want to do business with the government, these offices can point you in the right direction by informing you about who might need your services and how to apply.

Selling Overseas: Hitting foreign markets is essential to the success of most businesses. Certain state agencies are set up to help business people identify and sell to foreign markets.

Getting Federal Dollars: Most states have trained professionals who can direct business people toward federal loan and grant money.

Locating Private Investors: Many states are bringing together entrepreneurs with those wishing to invest capital. The states maintain data bases of prospective investors and set up programs that benefit both parties.

Enterprise Zones: Certain states set up these areas in which they try to encourage business development. Pro-business communities are selected to ensure long-term relationships between business and the local government. In these areas businesses will find expedited permit processing, reduced construction and permit-related fees and help in hiring and training employees. The state usually provides significant tax breaks as well as extensive assistance in areas such as marketing, research and development and business planning.

Program-Related Investments

Similar to a grant, a program-related investment (PRI) is an investment that a private foundation makes in a nonprofit organization, a profit-making business, or an individual that furthers the charitable objectives of the foundation (housing for low-income residents; expansion capital for a small manufacturing firm, which in turn will allow for the hiring of more workers; and so on). PRI's usually provide help in the form of direct loans, equity investments, letters of credit, outright grants, and/or donated services (which can range from copying equipment to consultants).

PRIs are invaluable sources of money for established businesses and, particularly, in start-up situations. Foundations will invest in some enterprises that many commercial investors would consider too speculative. They will act as patient investors, willing to wait through the difficult and often unprofitable early years of a businesses' life with the expectation that profits will come and the investment will pay an adequate return. The main function of the PRI, however, is to fulfill a major charitable objective. They are made directly to profit-making and non-profit businesses, as well as to individuals. Some foundations give only to non-profit organizations, which then administer the funds to others. In this case, an individual or business can use an established nonprofit corporation as a "flow-through," thereby eliminating the need to set up a separate non-profit corporation. The established non-profit foundation is usually given 3 to 5 percent of the money raised as a "flow-through fee."

Here are three examples of PRI grants; there is a complete state by state list included in the National Publications book *The Secrets Of Free Money.* (619) 543-9800.

The Luke B. Hancock Foundation
360 Bryant Street
Palo Alto, CA 94301
(415) 321-5536

Information: Funding is given primarily for job training and youth employment. Special project grants are awarded for situations that involve other foundations in areas where there is an

funding. Giving is limited to California, particularly the six counties of the San Francisco Bay Area.

Contact: Joan H. Wylie, Executive Director

Connecticut Mutual Life Foundation
140 Garden Street
Hartford, CT 06154
(203) 727-6500

Information: Grants are given for education, housing and employment programs. Money is administered for operating budgets, continuing support, seed money, building funds, matching funds, consulting services, technical assistance, program-related investments, special projects and conferences and seminars. Giving is focused primarily in the Hartford, Connecticut area.

Contact: Astrida R. Olds, Secretary

Charles K. Blandin Foundation
100 Pokegama Avenue North
Grand Rapids, MI 55744
(218) 326-0523

Information: Funding is provided for community projects and economic development. Money is designed for use in seed money, emergency funds, loans, program-related investments, special projects, consulting services, and technical assistance. Giving is limited to Minnesota, with emphasis on the north-eastern area.

Contact: Paul M. Olson, Executive Director

For further information, you can call the Foundation centers in New York at (212) 620-4230, in San Francisco as (415) 397-0902, and in Washington at (202) 331-1400).

Chapter Two

State Programs

Alabama

Small Business Development Centers
Alabama State University
915 South Jackson Street
Montgomery, AL 36195
(205) 269-1102

These centers offer free information and counseling to those who wish to start or expand their own business. These centers offer regular workshops and seminars on a wide variety of business-related topics and are located throughout the state. To find the one nearest you, contact the above address.

Alabama Development Office
State Capitol
Montgomery, AL 36130
(205) 263-0048

A source of information regarding industrial sites and buildings. Free individual counseling is provided to each individual from the start to the finish of their project. The information includes: Details involving labor sources, taxes and tax exemptions, financing and financial incentives, transportation, training, laws and regulations; information on natural resources, geography, climate, education and research and the quality of life in Alabama.

Alabama Development Office
Data Research Center
State Capitol
Montgomery, AL 36130.

(205) 263-0048

This agency prepares cost and feasibility studies for interested parties. Reports include information on natural resources, quality of life, demographics, economics, training and other subjects to meet individual needs.

(One Stop Permitting)
Alabama Development Office
Department of Environmental Management
State Capital
Montgomery, AL 36103
(205) 263-0048

All the permits for air, water and land can be obtained through this one agency.

Alabama Development Training
4505 Executive Park Drive
Montgomery, AL 36116
(205) 261-4158

This center conducts management training programs and seminars on other related topics.

(One Stop Financing)
Alabama Development Office
Industrial Finance Division
State Capitol
Montgomery, AL 36130
(205) 263-0048

This agency is a "one-stop" source for the funding of industrial finance. Qualified individuals assist clients in finding the most economical and efficient method of financing industrial locations or expansions.

Industrial Development Bond Issues
Industrial Finance Division
State Capitol
Montgomery, AL 36130
(205) 263-0048

These bonds can be used to purchase land, buildings, machinery and equipment for new industry and new additions for existing industry. Projects financed through IDB are 100 percent exempt from all property taxes for the entire length of the loan, which is normally 20 years. The interest rate is usually 70-85 percent of the prime lending rate. Financing is available up to 10 percent of the project cost.

Urban Development Action Grant
Industrial Finance Division
State Capitol
Montgomery, AL 36130
(205) 263-0048

Loans for the purchase of land, buildings, machinery, equipment and new expansions. The interest rate is below market. Grant is available only in certain communities and cannot exceed 1/4 of the project cost.

Alabama Development Office
(Industrial Finance Division)

Loans for land, buildings, machinery, equipment and new expansion. There is a $250,000 limit per project. The interest rate is normally two points below the prime. These loans can finance up to 40 percent of the project costs.

Small Business Administration (SBA) Loan 503
(Industrial Finance Division)

The bank loans 50 percent of the project cost and the SBA loans 40 percent of the project cost at below market rates.

State Industrial Site Preparation Grants
(Industrial Finance Division)

Helps manufacturing industries pay for industrial site preparation. May be used for conducting land and labor surveys and for grading, draining, and providing access to specific sites. The amount of the grant depends upon the amount of expenses for construction and equipment.

Speculating Building Revolving Loan Fund
(Industrial Finance Division)

Industrial development board may borrow up to 25 percent of the cost of constructing a speculative building for industrial development purposes with no interest on the money borrowed from the fund.

Alaska

Small Business Assistance Center
Courthouse Square
250 Cushman Street Suite 4-A
Fairbanks, AK 99701
(907) 451-8466

Provides assistance to qualified businesses, including: Business plans, marketing and feasibility studies and loan packages. This agency also provides additional assistance to minority construction businesses in the areas of: obtaining bonding, estimating, job specification review and bidding, and project management.

The AIDA Revenue Bond Financing Program
Alaska Industrial Development Authority
1577 C Street Suite 304
Anchorage, AK 99501-5177
(907) 274-1651

This program issues bonds for most types of commercial and industrial activity involving the construction of new plants and equipment, as well as acquisition. The borrower must locate a purchaser who agrees to buy 100 percent of the revenue bonds issued by AIDA for that project. The interest rates and other charges are determined jointly by the borrower and the lender.

AIDA Federally Guaranteed Loan Program
Alaska Industrial Development Authority
(Same address as above)

Loans to finance inventory, working capital, equipment and some refinancing of existing debt. AIDA will provide up to $500,000 by purchasing from the lender a participation in a loan that is guaranteed by the Federal Government. AIDA assesses no fees on these loans.

Arizona

Development Finance Program

Arizona Enterprise Development Corporation
Arizona Department of Commerce
1700 West Washington, 5th floor
Phoenix, AZ 85007
(602) 255-1782 or (602) 255-5705

This program provides loans to small expanding businesses through the SBA. The funds can be used for the purchase of land, buildings, machinery and equipment, construction, renovation and related expenses. Working capital, debt refinancing and consolidations are not eligible uses. Businesses must be for-profit and have generated an average net profit of less than two million dollars for each of the preceding two years, and have a total net worth of less than six million dollars. Companies must be located in Arizona, but outside of Phoenix and Tucson, which have their own programs. Interest rates are 3/4 percent above U.S. Treasury Bonds and the maximum loaned is $500,000. The loans are for a term of 15- to 25-years.

Revolving Loan Programs
Development Finance Unit
(See above address)

This program provides loans for economic development projects. The money can be used for site acquisition and improvements, construction, machinery and equipment, building rehabilitation and leasehold improvements. For-profit businesses located throughout Arizona (except Maricopa and Pima counties) are eligible. The interest rates are below market.

Arizona Department of Commerce
Financial Resources for Business Development

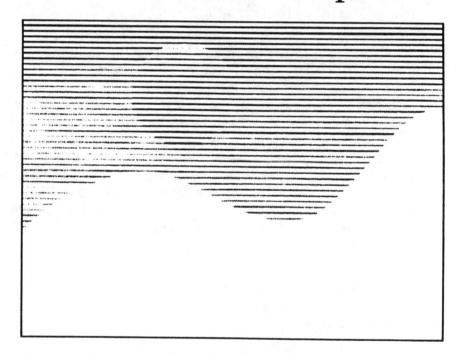

Urban Development Action Grants
Development Finance Unit
(See above address)

Used by certain cities, towns and all Indian reservations to provide subordinated loans to new and expanding businesses. The loans are usually for 10-20 percent of the project. Funds can be used for construction, improvements or rehabilitation of commercial, industrial and mixed-use developments. The purchase of machinery and equipment also is eligible. The terms and interest rate of the loan are negotiable.

Arkansas

Small Business Development Center
University of Arkansas at Little Rock
Central Office, Library,
5th floor, Room 512
33rd and University
Little Rock, AR 72204
(501) 371-5381
(Toll free in Arkansas: 1-800-482-5850 x5381)

These centers are located throughout the state to provide management assistance. Professional consultants work with clients on an individual basis. Start-up assistance as well as information regarding financial analysis, accounting, record keeping, business plans, management, and international trade for established businesses is available.

Minority Business Development Department
1 Capitol Mall
Room 4C-300
Little Rock, AR 72201
(501) 371-1060
This programs offers technical assistance and access to financial resources including a one-million-dollar **Minority Economic Development Fund** It also sponsors workshops and seminars

and assists minority businesses in obtaining government contracts.

Arkansas Industrial Development Commission
1 State Capitol Mall
Little Rock, AR 72201
(501) 371-7786

This program provides assistance for both start-up and existing businesses. Business must be at least three-years old. The maximum amount of an individual loan is $500,000.

California

Office of Local Development
California Department of Commerce
1121 L Street, Suite 600
Sacramento, CA 95814
(916) 322-1398

Provides case studies, seminars and other information on topics such as downtown redevelopment, industrial revitalization and financing.

Office of Business Development
California Department of Commerce
1121 L Street, Suite 600
Sacramento, CA 95814
(916) 322-5665

This office identifies available locations for business development in the state and provides information on regional economic trends, labor supply, wages, real estate prices, taxes, local regulations, etc. This office offers assistance in dealing with regulatory agencies.

Office of Small Business
1121 L Street Suite 600
Sacramento, CA 95814
(916) 327-4357

This agency provides sources of financing, consultation and business education assistance through workshops, seminars, individual counseling and informational materials. This office helps entrepreneurs locate organizations that will assist in all facets of business, including: the formulation of a business plan, marketing, management and sales strategy.

Small Business Development Centers

1121 L Street, Suite 600
California Department of Commerce
Sacramento, CA 95814
(916) 324-8102

The centers are located throughout the state to provide management and technical assistance, business information, marketing help, demographic data and assistance in rounding up federal, state and local aid. Call for the center nearest you.

Office of Small and Minority Business

Department of General Services
1808 14th Street, Suite 100
Sacramento, CA 95801
(916) 322-5060

This office offers assistance to businesses interested in securing state contracts.

California State Contact Register

Department of General Services
Office of Fiscal Services,
PO Box 151
Sacramento, CA 95801
(916) 322-5060

The Register is a bimonthly report on available state service and construction opportunities and commodity information. A one-year subscription is $60.

California Employment Development Department

800 Capitol Mall
Sacramento, CA 95814
(916) 445-8008

In offices around the state, these centers provide job listings and help employers qualify for federal and state tax credits for the hiring of individuals from certain targeted groups.

Job Training Partnership Office
800 Capitol Mall
Sacramento, CA 95814
(916) 445-4546

This office administers federal funds to train people on a local level. Job search assistance, retraining, relocation assistance, job development and other related training are all eligible uses.

Office of Permit Assistance
1400 10th Street
Sacramento, CA 95814
(916) 322-4245

A "One-Stop" agency for acquiring the necessary state permits. A *Permit Handbook* is available upon request which describes in detail over 40 major permits issued by state agencies for projects affecting the environment.

California Commission for Economic Development
Office of the Lieutenant Governor
State Capitol, Room 1028
Sacramento, CA 95814
(916) 445-8994

This agency provides information regarding requirements, regulations, forms, fees, and offices for use in establishing a business in the state of California. They publish a guide entitled: *Doing Business in California: A Guide for Establishing a Business.*

Employment Training Panel
Central Valley Office
800 Capitol Mall, MIC 64
Sacramento, CA 95814
(916) 324-3615

Provides funds to train workers in skills that a new or expanding small business may need. Trainees are selected by businesses from a large pool of experienced workers. Companies may either provide their own training or subcontract for it with a public or private school. Training can be in a classroom, laboratory or on the job.

Office of Local Development
California Department of Commerce
1121 L Street, Suite 600
Sacramento, CA 95814
(916) 322-1398

The Commerce Department administers a variety of state and federal loan and grant programs through this office. *A Funding Guide* is a publication that lists 260 funding sources. Some of the funding is available for: training and technical assistance, redevelopment and renovation of abandoned buildings and industrial sites.

California Innovation Development Loans
Office of Business Development
California Department of Commerce
1121 L Street, Suite 600
Sacramento, CA 95814
(916) 322-5665

This department provides direct loans to assist in the development of new technology. Businesses (and individuals) planning projects in deteriorated areas are eligible to apply for these loans. Funds must be used for the financing of fixed assets or working capital. Loans range for $100,000 to $500,000.

Small Business Loan Guarantees
Office of Business Development
(See above address)

This department has offices all over the state to provide loan guarantees to firms unable to secure conventional financing. The maximum guarantee can not exceed $350,000. Loan terms vary from one to seven years and usually at one to two points above the prime lending rate.

Industrial Development Bonds
Office of Business and Industrial Development
(See above address)

This office uses tax-exempt industrial development bonds to finance businesses wanting to locate or expand their operations.

Colorado

Business Information Center
Department of Regulatory Agency
Office of Regulatory Reform, Room 110
1525 Sherman Street
Denver, CO 80203
(303) 866-3933

This office provides information packages detailing licensing, regulations, permits, and taxes.

Small Business Assistance Center
Colorado Division of Commerce and Development
Department of Local Affairs
1313 SHerman Street, Room 523
Denver, CO 80203
(303) 866-2205
(Toll Free in Colorado: 1-800-521-1243.)

These centers are located around the state to provide information and assistance on: management, business plans, marketing and financing.

Office of Regulatory Reform
Department of Regulatory Agencies
1525 Sherman Street #110,
Denver, CO 80203
(303) 866-3933

Provides information and assistance for new businesses wishing to obtain the necessary licenses and permits.

Division of Purchasing
Department of Administration
1525 Sherman Street 7th Floor
Denver, CO 80203
(303) 866-2361

Assists small businesses in getting government contracts.

Minority Business Development Center
428 East 11th Avenue
Denver, CO 80203
(303) 832-2228

This agency offers assistance in the following areas: consulting, marketing, procurement of government contracts, management and employee training and other related services.

Colorado Business Development Agency
Division of Commerce and Development
1313 Sherman Street, Room 523
Denver, CO 80203
(303) 866-2205

This program loans money for working capital and refinancing, equipment and building expansion and offers guaranteed financing for exporting businesses.

Farmers Home Administration
2490 West 26th Avenue
Denver, CO 80211
(303) 964-0151

This agency guarantees loans in non-metropolitan areas of Colorado. Guarantees up to 90 percent of a loan from a bank or other lender for any kind of business that benefits a rural community.

Division of Commerce and Development
1313 Sherman Street, Room 523
Denver, CO 80203
(303) 866-2205

This office assists in financing small businesses which will create jobs for low- and moderate-income people. Maximum loan amount is $100,000 and businesses must be located in communities with a population of less than 50,000.

Connecticut

Connecticut Small Business Development Center
University of Connecticut
39 Woodland Street
Hartford, CT 06105
(203) 241-4982

This agency has offices all over the state geared toward assisting prospective businesspeople establish new firms.

Small Business Office
Connecticut Department of Economic Development
210 Washington Street
Hartford, CT 06106
(203) 566-4051

Provides individual attention to businesses just starting up or trying to expand. Information is available regarding: business plans, marketing, expansion, management advice and other related topics.

Connecticut Technology Assistance Center
Connecticut Department of Economic Development
210 Washington Street
Hartford, CT 06106
(203) 566-4051

This agency provides information on all private and public services, programs and resources available to help high- technology companies establish and grow in Connecticut.

Local Business Development Organizations
Office of Small Business Affairs
Connecticut Department of Economic Development
210 Washington Street
Hartford, CT 06106
(203) 566-4051

Provides organizational, administrative, managerial, financial and other related help to minority businesspeople. Call for the location nearest you.

Business Resource Centers
Business Resource Centers
Office of Small Business Affairs
Connecticut Department of Economic Development
210 Washington Street
Hartford, CT 06106
Phone: (203) 566-4051

Description: These centers fill the gap between the Local Business Development Organizations and the private sector. They assist businesspeople in locating sources of funding, promoting markets for goods and services, and creating new business opportunities.

Industrial Revenue Bonds
Connecticut Development Authority
217 Washington Street
Hartford, CT 06106
Phone: (203) 522-3730

Description: Provides long-term industrial revenue bond financing to cover the purchase and development of land; construction and purchase of new buildings or remodeling of existing ones; purchase of machinery and equipment; and the purchase and installation of pollution control and environmental protection equipment. Types of projects funded include manufacturing, processing, assembling, research facilities, offices, warehousing and certain recreational facilities.

Connecticut Product Development Corporation
Connecticut Product Development Corporation
78 Oak Street
Hartford, CT 06106
Phone: (203) 566-2920
Description: Assists in the development of new products and procedures by Connecticut businesses in cases where funding cannot be obtained through other sources. Also provides assistance to businesses working in joint ventures with Connecticut firms.

Delaware

Delaware Small Business Development Centers
Delaware Small Business Development Centers
Bureau of Economic and Business Research
005 Purnell Hall
Newark, DE 19716
Phone: (302) 451-2747 (Toll-free for Kent and Sussex counties, call 1-800-222-2279)

Description: Management and technical training and assistance is offered to small businesses at no cost.

Environmental Permitting
Department of Natural Resources and Environmental Control
Development Advisory Service
89 Kings Highway
PO Box 1401
Dover, DE 19903
Phone: (302) 736-5409

Description: Assistance is available for coordination and preparation prior to the review process necessary for numerous government permits. Applicants will meet with state and local government representatives to be advised about permits and other requirements that may be applicable to their projects. The applicants will also receive a letter detailing the necessary requirements.

Delaware Energy Office
Delaware Energy Office, Small Business Program
Margaret M. O'Neill Building
Dover, DE 19901
Phone: (302) 736-5644 (Toll-free hotline in Delaware, call 1-800-282-8616)

Description: Provides free on-site energy efficiency evaluations for small businesses. Also offers workshops and seminars on controlling energy costs and conservation measures for businesses.

Delaware State Chamber of Commerce
Delaware State Chamber of Commerce
One Commerce Center, Suite 200
Wilmington, DE 19801
Phone: (302) 655-7221

Description: Provides information to small businesses concerning finance and banking through special programs and "Small Business Financing Traveling Road Shows."

Industrial Revenue Bonds
Delaware Development Office
99 Kings Highway
PO Box 1401
Dover, DE 19903
Phone: (302) 736-4271

Description: Provides long-term, low-interest loans to finance fixed assets in industrial, commercial, agricultural, and pollution control fields. Loans are limited to a maximum of $10 million for each project except for pollution control projects where there are no maximums.

District of Columbia

Small Business Development Center
Howard University Small Business Development Center
School of Business and Public Administration
Georgia Avenue and Fairmont Street, NW
Howard University
Washington, DC 20059
Phone: (202) 636-5150

Description: Free services include: Technical assistance; management counseling; management training; research, publications, and information services; special projects and financial facilitation.

Minority Business Opportunity Commission
Minority Business Opportunity Commission
613 G Street, NW

Room 926
Washington, DC 20001
Phone: (202) 727-3818

Description: Offers assistance and information on district government procurement opportunities, seminars on district government resources, and information on private sector contracting.

"One-Stop" Business and Permit Center

District of Columbia Department of Consumer and Regulatory Affairs
614 H Street, NW
Washington, DC 20001
Phone: (202) 727-7100

Description: Provides information as well as processing business licences and permits.

National Development Council

1025 Connecticut Avenue, NW
Washington, DC 20004
Phone: (202) 466-3906

Description: Responsible for administering the Small Business Revitalization Program, a federally sponsored plan for mobilizing private sector capital for small businesses and industries.

Revolving Loan Fund

District of Columbia Office of Business and Economic Development
1350 Pennsylvania Avenue, NW
Room 208
Washington, DC 20004
Phone: (202) 727-6600

Description: Administers loan funds to be used in coordination with private capital with terms ranging from 30 days to 2 years. These funds are used for short-term gap financing.

Florida

Small Business Development Centers
Small Business Development Center
Tallahassee Small Business Regional Center
1605 East Plaza Drive
Tallahassee, FL 32308
Phone: (904) 644-6524

Description: Offers free training and individual counseling on such aspects of business as: Financial and accounting analysis; commercial loan packages; market analysis; steps to starting a business; personnel management; international trade; business plans; feasibility studies; inventor and innovation assistance.

Florida Department of Commerce
Florida Department of Commerce
Bureau of Business Assistance
107 West Gaines Street
Suite G-26, Collins Building
Tallahassee, FL 32301
Phone: (904) 488-9357

Description: Provides direct assistance and referrals in matters concerning: Labor force, marketing and production, plant start-up and expansion, legislative updates, statistical and information-al data, and community development.

Florida First Capital Finance Corporation, INC.
Florida First Capital Finance Corporation, INC.
PO Box 5826
Tallahassee, FL 32301
Phone: (904) 487-0466

Description: Funds are used for land acquisition, building construction, purchase, renovation, or modernization, and machinery and equipment. FFCFC is authorized to sell debentures with SBA guarantees up to 40% of eligible project cost with a $500,000 ceiling. The bank portion of the loan will be at the market interest rate, while the SBA portion of the loan will be three-quarters of one percent above the long-term treasury bond rate of comparable term at time of closing. A minimum term of 10 years is required by private lenders. Loan terms are 15, 20, and 25 years on the SBA portion of the loan, depending on the useful life of assets and terms of private lender.

Georgia

Small Business Development Centers
Small Business Development Center
Georgia State University, Suite 1055
1 Park Place South
Atlanta, GA 30303
Phone: (404) 658-3550

Description: Free information and counseling is available to small businesses regarding financial planning, sales techniques, display and advertising, market evaluation, risk management, organization structure, inventory control, refinancing, exporting, and starting a business.

Community Development Block Grants
Georgia Department of Community Affairs
Community and Economic Development Division
40 Marietta Street, NW
Suite 800
Atlanta, GA 30303
Phone: (404) 656-3839

Description: Communities must apply for funding and selected businesses receive funding for development from the community. Also provides referrals to other sources.

Hawaii

Small Business Information Service
Small Business Information Service
Hawaii Department of Planning and Economic Development
250 South King Street, Room 724
Honolulu, HI 96813

Phone: (808) 548-7645 (Toll-free for out of state, call Sprint- access seven-digit number + 617-5553)

Description: Provides free information and referrals to anyone interested in starting or expanding a small business. Programs are available for increasing sales, improving profitability and expanding employment in Hawaii. Also provides businesses with information on the following: Permits and licensing, market data, business plan writing services, consulting services, government procurement, alternative financing, and business classes.

Hawaii Entrepreneur Training and Development Institute
Hawaii Entrepreneur Training and Development Institute
1750 Kalakaua Avenue, Suite 1409
Honolulu, HI 96813
Phone: (808) 955-8655 (Cable: HETADI)

Description: Offers management and technical training and assistance for entrepreneurs and small businesses in Hawaii and other countries. Their services include business plan writing, marketing studies, feasibility analysis and loan proposal preparation.

Hawaii Island Economic Development Board
Hawaii Island Economic Development Board
First Federal Building
75-5737 Kuakini Highway, #206
Kailua-Kona, HI 96740
Phone: (808) 329-4713

Description: Provides support for start-up and established businesses in locating operations on the island of Hawaii. This support is given in the form of development of plans, coordination of fixed asset financing with local financial institutions and the Small Business Administration, providing information on permitting, zoning, and other governmental rules and regulations, and providing site selection information.

Kauai Economic Development Board
Kauai Economic Development Board
4370 Kukui Grove Street, Suite 211-C
Lihue, HI 96766
Phone: (808) 245-6692

Description: Provides a pool of information and assists sole proprietorships as well as corporations. Entrepreneurs can receive assistance in securing financing, site selection, and state and county business permits and regulations. Statistics, studies, and other business information can also be obtained through this service.

Small Business Center
Small Business Center
Hawaii Chamber of Commerce
735 Bishop Street
Honolulu, HI 96813
Phone: (808) 531-4111

Description: The Hawaii Chamber of Commerce sponsors this center which offers a wide range of services to small businesses. The Small Business Centers provide entrepreneur training, business consulting, financial assistance and loan packaging, and information and referral services. Special training programs are also offered to entrepreneurs who show potential for creating their own viable business.

Pacific Business Center Program
Pacific Business Center Program
University of Hawaii at Manoa
BUSAD D-202
2404 Maile Way
Honolulu, HI 96822
Phone: (808) 948-6286

Description: Encourages the transfer of information and technology between university research departments and the private industries in Hawaii and American Flag Pacific Islands. The Center maintains a catalog of faculty consultants who can provide small business with advice and assistance ranging from financial planning and communication skills to operations research and engineering. These various services are available free to program clients. Consulting with faculty is available for a nominal service charge.

Hawaii Employers Council
Hawaii Employers Council
2682 Waiwai Loop
Honolulu, HI 96819
Phone: (808) 836-1511

Description: Offers counseling, assistance, and information on such areas of employee management as personnel administration, supervisory training, industrial relations, contract negotiation, and counter-organizing.

Alu Like, INC.
ALU LIKE-Oahu
1316 Kaumualii Street
Honolulu, HI 96817

Phone: (808) 848-1486

Description: Provides technical and consultant support to Hawaiian-owned businesses, prospective entrepreneurs, and community economic enterprise developments. The state office deals with community economic enterprise developments, while the Multi-Service Centers deal with business start-ups and expansions.

Maui Economic Development Board, INC.
Maui Economic Development Board, INC.
PO Box 187
Kahului, HI 96723
Phone: (808) 877-3839

Description: Develops programs to enhance the diversity of Maui's economy. The board is currently engaged in developing a Research and Technology Park for new and innovative small businesses. They also have established several Continuing Action Panels to help entrepreneurs share experiences and information in fields such as agriculture, electronics, aquiculture, and research and development. Offers conferences and information about topics of interest to small businesses.

Honolulu Job Training Program
Honolulu Job Training Program
715 South King Street, 5th Floor
Honolulu, HI 96813
Phone: (808) 523-4221

Description: Funds are available for industry-based training designed for a company or group of similar companies to reduce training and labor costs through tax credits and incentives. Allows a company to use its own training methods to teach its own personnel.

Small Business Hawaii
811-A Cooke Street,
Honolulu, HI 96813
(808) 545-4533
This organization provides education and advisory and counseling services. It publishes a monthly newsletter, "Small Business News," and sponsors a bimonthly publication, "Share and Tell Business Forums."

Hawaii Business League
1177 Kapiolani Boulevard, Suite 201
Honolulu, HI 96814
(808) 533-6819

Programs provide information on current issues, including IRS rules and regulations as they affect small businesses.

State Permit Information Counter
Hawaii Department of Planning and Economic Development,
Room 610, Sixth Floor, Kamamalu Building
250 South King Street
Honolulu, HI 96813
(808) 548-8467

Provides information on state land and water-use permits required by the state or federal government.

Industry and Product Promotion Program
Small Business Information Service
Hawaii Department of Planning and Economic Development
250 South King Street

Honolulu, HI 96813
(808) 548-7645 or (808) 548-7887
Offers state help (including financial assistance) to local manufacturers for promoting Hawaiian products.

Hawaii Capital Loan Program

Small Business Information Service
Hawaii Department of Planning and Economic Development
250 South King Street, Room 724
Honolulu, HI 96813
(808) 548-7645

Provides loans to small businesses for construction, conversion or expansion, land acquisition and machinery, supplies and other equipment. Applicants must be unable to obtain financing elsewhere.

Idaho

Idaho Business Development Centers

Boise State University
Idaho Business Development Center
1910 University Drive
Boise, ID 83725
(208) 385-1640

These centers provide assistance for a variety of technical purposes relating to starting a business in Idaho, including counseling, training, and research assistance. Most services are free.

Certified Development Company Loans

US Small Business Administration
1020 Main Street, Suite 290
Boise, ID 83702
(208) 334-1780

These loans are long term and fixed rate and offered mostly for expansion of already existing businesses. Maturity is up to 25 years.

Illinois

Small Business Development Centers
Statewide Program Administrator
Business Assistance Office
620 East Adams
Springfield, IL 62701
(217) 785-6174 (In Illinois: 1-800-252-2923)

Small business advice and assistance in the areas of government procurement, exporting, business skills, and market conditions. Contact the above address for the location nearest you.

Teltapes
Department of Commerce and Community Affairs
620 East Adams
Springfield, IL 62701
(217) 785-6162

A series of taped phone messages covering a wide range of subjects having to do with doing business in Illinois. The number (in Illinois only) is 1-800-835-3222.

One Stop Permit Center
Illinois Department of Commerce and Community Affairs
Business Assistance Office
620 East Adams Street, Third Floor
Springfield, IL 62701
(217) 785-6162
Toll Free in Illinois: 1-800-252-2923

Provides information to new and existing businesses on all state government forms and applications. Also distributes a business start-up kit.

Friends of Small Business
225 West Randolph, HQ 30C
Chicago, IL 60606
(312) 727-3225

Provides businesspeople with an exchange of ideas and oppor-

Envision Hawaii!

dbed
DEPARTMENT OF BUSINESS
AND ECONOMIC DEVELOPMENT

CHECKLIST
FOR
EMPLOYERS
IN HAWAII

*FOR HELP AND INFORMATION IN OBTAINING BUSINESS
LICENSES AND PERMITS, CALL OR VISIT:*

BusinessActionCenter

Department of Business and Economic Development
1130 North Nimitz Highway, Suite A 254
Honolulu, Hawaii 96817
Phone: (808) 543-6691
Neighbor Islands Toll Free Number: 1-800-225-6723
FAX: (808) 543-6699

Small Business Information Service

tunities.

Illinois Venture Fund
Marketing Staff
Illinois Department of Commerce and Community Affairs
620 East Adams Street
Springfield, IL 62701
(217) 782-1460

Provides equity capital for new businesses located in the state. Investments will take the form of common stock or securities which convert to common stock.

Illinois Development Finance Authority - Direct Loan Fund
Illinois Department of Commerce and Community Affairs
(See above address.)

Provides fixed-rate loans for small or medium-sized industrial or manufacturing firms that cannot meet all their financial requirements from conventional sources and is intended to create jobs in areas of high unemployment.

Build Illinois Small Business Development Program
(Illinois Department of Commerce and Community Affairs
(See above address.)

Provides direct financing to small businesses for expansion. Designed to promote job creation and retention.

Indiana

Indiana Institute For New Business Ventures, INC.
One North Capitol, Suite 501, Indianapolis, IN 46204
(317) 634-8418

This organization creates a network inclusive of: education, management, technical and financial resources with professional experience to counsel the fledgling businessman on his venture. This organization introduces businesses to the appropriate funding sources: state loan guarantee programs, venture capitalist commercial banks, individual investors, seed capital funds, Small Business Investment Corporations and Certified Development Corporations. This organization also hosts a number of one-to-one programs designed for the emerging businessman. These include : Capital Formation Matching Grants; Indiana Seed Capital Network, Enterprise Advisory Service, The Indiana Emerging Business Forum, and Small Business Counselors.

Indiana Department of Administration
Minority Business Development
100 North Senate Avenue, Room 502
Indianapolis, IN 46204
(317) 232-3061

Assists minority businesses in bidding on procurement awards from the state of Indiana.

Iowa

Small Business Advisory Council
Iowa Development Commission
600 East Court Ave.
Des Moines, IA 50309
Small Business Division
515-281-8310 or 515-281-8324 (Toll-free number in Iowa: 1-800-532-1216).

A council that acts in a "guru-like" manner, providing assistance and guidance at the start-up, duration, and growth of small businesses. Their services include: referrals, technical assistance, sources of financial assistance, training in marketing products or services to the government, educational programs that pertain to individuals interested in business. Acts as a forum that reviews complaints submitted by small businesses which concern rules made by state agencies. Also provides other information.

Call One

Iowa Development Commission
600 East Court Avenue
Des Moines, IA 50309

A source for small business information. It has a toll free number which you can call for responses to immediate questions and concerns for small businesses (1-800-532-1216). This number will also direct specific requests to existing programs that have available resources. If staff members cannot answer your question immediately, they will contact you within five working days with the answer. (515)-281-8310.

Iowa Development Commission

600 East Court Avenue, Suite A
Des Moines, IA 50309
(515)-281-3925 (Toll-free number in Iowa: 1-800-532-1216)
Venture Capital

This source of funding is not a loan. It is a program in which investors take an equity position in the company. Companies viewed as high risk often opt for this form of investment.

Iowa Product Development Corporation

600 East Court Avenue Suite A
Des Moines, IA 50309
(515)-281-3925 (toll-free number in Iowa:1-800-532-1216)

These are funds for a product or project that is considered to have a high risk potential, which therefore, would not be supported by a commercial institution. Preference given to agriculture-related applicants, or businesses in an area that the board decides has been affected by depressed agricultural prices, or an applicant who submits an invention that will shift the business to nonagricultural related industrial or commercial activity.

Iowa Business Development Credit Corporation

901 Insurance Exchange Building
Fifth and Grand
Des Moines, IA 50309
(515) 282-2164

Loans up to $500,000 extended to firms that lack collateral or financial backing for conventional loans. Interest rates will be set at the "going rate" for this type of credit. The "pay back" schedule may stretch out over 15 years.

US Small Business Administration Guaranteed Loans
US Small Business Administration Loan Officer
749 Federal Building
Des Moines, IA 50309
(515) 284-4422

The SBA will guarantee a loan from a private lender, or a bank. Guaranty may reach 90 percent or $500,000, which ever is the lesser amount. Loan conditions and terms are negotiated between the lender and the borrower.

Iowa Finance Authority
550 Liberty Building
418 Sixth Avenue
Des Moines, IA 50309
515-284-4422

The Iowa Finance Authority assists the development and expansion of small business. They do this through the sale of bonds and notes which are not federally taxed. The proceeds provide limited financing for new or existing small businesses (less than $3 million in sales or having less than 20 employees defines the term "small business"). The maximum loan extended is $10 million. This money may not be used for working capital, inventory or operating purposes; it may be used for purchasing land, construction, building improvements or equipment.

Kansas

"One-Stop" Clearinghouse
One-Stop Permitting, Development Division
Kansas Department of Economic Development
503 Kansas Avenue, Sixth Floor
Topeka, KS 66603
913-296-3483.

This office has all the necessary state applications required by licensing agencies, and information regarding taxes. They have all the information necessary to establish, or operate a business. They answer questions about establishing and developing a business in Kansas.

College of Business Administration

Kansas State University
Calvin Hall
Manhattan, KS 66506
(913) 532-5529

A Small Business owner is matched with a group of university and college business majors. They meet regularly. Hypothetical situations in business are discussed and suggested solutions submitted. It is a program to make the business knowledge gained in a scholastic environment applicable to today's world.

Center for Entrepreneurship

And Small Business Management
College of Business Administration
Wichita State University
130 Clinton Hall, Box 88
Wichita, KS 67208
316-689-3000

Information bank with library and publications which are available to students, professors, and practitioners. Organizes, develops, and conducts seminars for practicing entrepreneurs, small business managers, and special interest groups.

Small Business Development Centers

College of Business Administration
Wichita State University
130 Clinton Hall, Box 88
Wichita, KS 67208
316-689-3367
Help entrepreneurs through services that disseminate business management information, management audits, financial analysis, feasibility studies, market studies, and business planning.

Small Business Education

Community Economic Development
Division of Cooperative Extension Service
Kansas State University
Umberger Hall, Room 115

MARYLAND

Guide To
Business
Regulations

Maryland
Department of Economic &
Employment Development

GUIDE TO STARTING
A BUSINESS
IN KANSAS

Kansas Department of Commerce
Division of Existing Industry Development
400 West Eighth Street, Fifth Floor
Topeka, Kansas 66603-3957
913-296-5298

October, 1987

Manhattan, KS 66506
(913) 532-5840

Organization that provides basic educational courses for small business groups. They also offer seminars and workshops to help small business managers increase sales, motivate employees, improve record keeping, study trade areas, and deal with inadequate financing, cash flow and accounts receivable problems.

Business and Engineering Technical Applications Program (BETA)
BETA Space Technology Center
University of Kansas
2291 Irving Hill Drive Campus West
Lawrence, KS 66045
913-864-4775

Provides technical information that pertains to a company's business. They assist business and industry administrative problems by providing this information.

Minority Business Division
Kansas Department of Economic Development
503 Kansas Avenue Sixth Floor
Topeka, KS 66603
(913) 296-3805

Technical assistance given with preference towards minorities and women seeking to start, develop, or improve a business.

Business Development Division
Economic Development Administration
Rocky Mountain Regional Office
333 West Colfax Avenue, Station 300
Denver, CO 80202
(303)-837-4474
This financial assistance is limited to designated areas or development districts. These monies come in the form of direct loans, loan guarantees of rental repayments of leases in order to solve job and income problems in areas of high unemployment or low family income, and purchase of evidences of indebtedness.

Minority Enterprises Small Business Investment Company
Central Systems Equity Corporation,
1743 North Hillside
Wichita, KS 67214
(316)-683-9004

Capital in the form of debt and equity loans to be applied towards the purchase of equipment, debt restructuring, business expansion and acquisition of shareholder or partnership interest.

Kansas Development Credit Corporation, Inc.
First National Bank Towers, Suite 1030
Topeka, KS 66603
(913) 235-3437

Small Businesses that meet SBA requirements are eligible for a loan up to $200,000. Money can be for purchasing equipment, working capital, expanding the business, acquiring shareholder or partner interest, and debt restructuring.

Kansas Development Credit Corporation, Inc.
First National Bank Towers, Suite 1030
Topeka, KS 66603
(913) 235-3437

This organization obtains funds from more than 400 Kansas member banks. These loans are for companies that had problems securing monetary assistance from conventional lenders and range up to $200,000.

Kentucky

Business Information Clearinghouse,
Kentucky Department of Economic Development
Commerce Cabinet, 22nd Floor
Capital Plaza Tower
Frankfort, KY 40601
(502) 564-4252
(Toll-free number in Kentucky: 1-800-626-2250)

Assistance offered to all new and existing businesses, regardless of the size, type, or location. At this location, you have access to the permit and license applications you will need to establish a business. It is a center for business information. It also makes referrals to government financial and management assistance programs and serves as a regulatory reform advocate for business.

Small Business Division

Kentucky Department of Economic Development
Commerce Cabinet
Capital Plaza Tower, 22nd Floor
Frankfort, KY 40601
(502)-564-4252

The following information pertains to existing and prospective small business owners/managers. This organization supplies information and referrals. It will prepare applications for the Commonwealth Small Business Development Corporation 503 Financial Assistance Loan Program and the Kentucky Development Finance Authority Financial Assistance Loan Program. They will cooperate with the small business community in promoting, developing and retaining small businesses. Offers counseling and entrepreneurial training and follow up, which provides management and technical assistance. Will direct entrepreneur to local sources of assistance. Encourages community to include small business as an integral part of their growth. Provides information on methods, services, and resources that will help the small business owner achieve his goals. Their services are not on a one-to-one basis.

Industrial Development and Marketing Division

Kentucky Department of Economic Development,
2300 Capital Plaza Tower
Frankfort, KY 40601
(502)-564-7140

This organization offers confidential, technical and professional expertise to existing and fledgling entrepreneurs. This includes services like plant location assistance.

Blue Grass State Skills Corporation, Room 2135

Capital Plaza Tower
Frankfort, KY 40601
(502) 564-3472

At little or no cost to the industrial employer, workers will be trained to a certain skill level as specified by the employer.

Minority Business Division
Kentucky Department of Economic Development, Commerce Cabinet,
2222 Capital Plaza Tower
Frankfort, KY 40601
(502)-564-2064

Supports and advocates the development, and expansion of minority businesses through resources made available in services offered by the state. These include: education, training, and assistance in public sector purchasing for minority business enterprise.

SBA 503 Loan Program
Kentucky Development Finance Authority, 24th Floor
Capital Plaza Tower
Frankfort, KY 40601
(502)-564-4554

Offers funds which may provide up to 40 percent of the total of an expansion project. The term of this loan spans 25 years at a fixed interest rate. The ceiling amount for the SBA is $500,000 per project. The projects selected usually range between $100,000 to $5 million, although projects under $100,000 will be considered. The program is designed to help already established businesses with a healthy customer base.

KDFA Direct Loan Program
Kentucky Development Finance Authority, 24th floor
Capital Plaza Tower,
Frankfort KY 40601
(502)-564-4554

Program designed to support the long term financing required to encourage expansion. It is a mortgage loan to supplement private financing. The financed projects are limited to agribusiness, tourism, or industrial ventures. These loans range from $25,000 to $250,000. Their requirements include that the project must create new jobs or have a financial impact on the community. Interest rate is based on the term of the loan; for example,
10 year loan = 5%
15 year loan = 6.4%
20 year loan = 7%

Industrial Revenue Bond Issue Program
Kentucky Development Finance Authority, 24th floor
Capital Plaza Tower
Frankfort, KY 40601
(502)-564-4554

This program is designed for financially strong companies. If they qualify, they may take advantage of tax-exempt rates of interest. Eligible projects will be issued bonds. The local government must ask the KDFA to issue the bond. There is an issuing fee of .1% of the amount charged. The maximum rate that can be charged is %10 with an additional application fee of $350.

Louisiana

Small Business Development Center
NLU Small Business Development Center
College of Business Administration
Northeast Louisiana University
Monroe, LA 71209 318-342-2129

This is an information and resource center for the 12 northeast Louisiana parishes. They offer management and technical assistance, education, and counseling. There may be a small fee charged for workshops or seminars.

Cost Free Training
Louisiana Department of Commerce
PO Box 94185
Baton Rouge, LA 70804
(504)-342-5361

At no cost to the company, a start-up training program is designed by the Office of Commerce and Industry. In consultation with company production officials, the office studies the plant site area and develops manuals and training films. They will provide materials and equipment, and they will hire instructors. The Office of Commerce and Industry then schedules some training sessions, and they recruit trainees who will attend the classes on their own time and without pay. The company has complete control over who they hire.

Industrial Revenue Bonds
Louisiana Department of Commerce
PO Box 94185
Baton Rouge, LA 70804
(504)-342-5361

These bonds are issued by local authorities, public trusts and development boards. The maximum amount is $10 million and are tax-exempt revenue bonds. The stipulation involved is that the money must finance the construction, expansion, or equipping of new industrial facilities. The business owners then lease the facilities and equipment at a fee that will retire the bonds. At the end of the lease period, the company may either purchase the facility or continue to lease at a low rate.

Louisiana Minority Business Development Authority
PO Box 44185
Baton Rouge, LA 70804
(504)-342-5359

Encourages business opportunities through loans that fund minority business.

Maine

New Enterprise Institute
Center for Research and Advanced Study
University of Southern Maine
246 Deering Avenue
Portland, ME 04102
(207)-780-4420

This is a research and development project. It offers businesspeople the opportunity to utilize these services: education, management assistance and information on administration, marketing and technology. They also have a small Business Development Center.

Maine Development Foundation
One Memorial Circle
Augusta, ME 04330
207-622-6345

This is a non-profit organization established by state legislation. Under this law, education, government, and business leaders work together pooling their resources to stimulate small Business enterprise in Maine. Professional assistance is available in such areas as: joint public/private development projects, industrial and commercial real estate development, business financing, location and financing of industrial and commercial facilities, export market development, securing public assistance and approvals, legislation development.

Maine State Development Office
193 State Street
Augusta, ME 04333
(207) 289-2656.

This organization encourages the development and expansion of already existing businesses, in addition to promoting and recruiting new industries to the state. Their services embrace the following elements: site location, technical, business, export, financial packaging, training and the Community Industrial Building Fund.

Umbrella Bond Program
Finance Authority of Maine
State House, Augusta, ME 04333
(207) 289-3095

This is a loan with the maximum amount set at $1 million. The loan is distributed to individuals and small businesses who will apply it towards establishing new or expanding existing businesses. Business owners must be involved with fishing, manufacturing, agricultural, industrial, or recreational ventures within Maine. The interest rates will be determined upon the sale of the bond. The loan term may not exceed 25 years. If the loan is for industrial and agricultural machinery and equipment, its term may not exceed 10 years.

Maryland

Small Business Development Center
College of Business and Management

University of Maryland
College Park, MD 20742
(301)-454-5072

The free services offered by this center include: research, financial facilitation, management, technical assistance, counseling, publications and information. This is not a source of funding, but rather a liaison between university business majors and the private sector.

Maryland Business Assistance Center

45 Calvert Street
Annapolis, MD 21401
(301) 269-2945
(Toll free number in Maryland 1-800-OK-Green)

The above toll-free line is the state's program. It is a hot line that will connect the caller with programs and services designed to assist businesses' development and expansion. These services include: flexible public financing, selling to the government, foreign trade zones, state funded employee training, enterprise zones, and the licensing and permit process.

Department of Economic and Community Development

Maryland Business Assistance Center
45 Calvert Street
Annapolis, MD 21401
(301) 269-2945
(Toll free number in Maryland 1-800-OK-Green)

Confidentially, a financial specialist will work with a company and help evaluate its needs. The specialist will also identify available resources. This department provides businesses with a selection of financing alternatives. The loans vary from $35,0000 to $10 million. The interest rates vary with each loan. Maturity of the loan spans up to 30 years.

Development Credit Fund, INC.

1925 Eutaw Place
Baltimore, MD 21217
(301) 523-6400

Geared toward minority-owned companies, this program provides below-market financing (in Maryland, of course).

Massachusetts

Call One Business Service Center
Massachusetts Department of Commerce and Development
100 Cambridge Street
Boston, MA 02202
(617)-727-4005
(Toll-free number in Massachusetts: 1-800-632-8181)

This is a "hot line" which is a direct and toll-free line. It offers information and assistance on many business subjects. These topics include: demographics, permit and licensing regulations, hourly wages and taxes.

Small Business Assistance Division
Massachusetts Department of Commerce and Development
100 Cambridge Street
Boston, MA 02202
(617)-727-4005

An Organization which provides a "one-stop" shop for businesses already in existence, and to those people wanting to start a business. The services housed in this organization include: management, financial and technical assistance.

Massachusetts Small Business Development Centers
Massachusetts Department of Commerce and Development
100 Cambridge Street
Boston, MA 02202
(617)-727-4005
(Toll-free number in Massachusetts: 1-800-632-8181)

This organization offers free counseling on a one-to-one basis. They evaluate the specific needs of the client and direct them toward services that would satisfy these needs. They are also an educational institute, in that they hold seminars, workshops, and conferences. At these gatherings, a variety of business topics are explored and discussed. A nominal fee may be charged for training. In addition, there are some Specialty Centers which focus on certain services. Some are: Technology, Minority Business Training and Resource Center, Productivity and Innovation Center, and Capital Formation Service.

Site Inventory Tracking Exchange (SITE)
Massachusetts Department of Commerce
100 Cambridge Street
Boston, MA 02202
(617)-727-3215

Industrial land and building space are maintained in a computer by this organization. Their printout is a comprehensive list that includes the sites attributes. Firms, in-state and out-of-state, who would like to start-up, expand, or relocate may request this free service.

Massachusetts Small Business Purchasing
Small Business Assistance
Massachusetts Department of Commerce
100 Cambridge Street
Boston, MA 02202
(617)-727-4005

A weekly publication called, "The Goods and Services Bulletin," contains information about bidding on state contracts. This service will also assist businesses participating in state purchasing.

State Office Of Minority Business Assistance (SOMBA)
Massachusetts Department of Commerce
100 Cambridge Street
Boston, MA 02202
(617)-727-8692

Geared toward supplying services to minorities and women-owned businesses, this service will increase access to public construction work. They also offer the following services - education and training, information and referral, and advocacy.

Massachusetts Industrial Finance Agency (MIFA)
125 Pearl Street
Boston, MA 02110
(617)-451-2477

The sales of industrial revenue bonds, loan guarantees, and pollution control bonds as a means of promoting employment growth. Financing commercial real estate, in locally identified Commercial Area Revitalization Districts (CARD), is possible with MIFA funds.

Massachusetts Technology Development Corporation (MTDC)
84 State Street, Suite 500
Boston, MA 02109
617-723-4920

This program is designed to provide capital to expanding and new technological companies. To qualify for this funding, these companies must have the potential to create significant employment growth in the Massachusetts area. MTDC will invest a minimum of $100,000 and a maximum of $250,000. MTDC teams up with partners from the private sector who usually invest two to four times the amount of the capital that MTDC provides.

Massachusetts Community Development Finance Corporation

131 State Street, Suite 600
Boston, MA 02109
(617) 742-0366

This program is designed to finance working capital needs and real estate development projects if it is evident that the public will gain from these undertakings. There are three different programs for investment in economic development projects: Community Development Investment Program, Venture Capital Investment Program and Small Loan Guarantee Program.

Massachusetts Business Development Corporation

One Boston Place
Boston, MA 02108
(617) 723-7515

This is the place for businesses that could not secure financial backing from conventional sources. MBDC offer up to 100 percent financing through medium and long term loans. Their types of loans include: working capital, second mortgages, leveraged buy-outs, government guaranteed loans, SBA 503 loans and long-term for new equipment or energy conversion.

Massachusetts Capital Resource Company (MCRC)

545 Boylston Street
Boston, MA 02116
(617)-536-3900
Almost any Massachusetts-based company can qualify for MCRC investments which range from $100,000 to $5 million. They back traditional as well as technology based industries. They also invest in management buy-outs, high-risk start-up companies, business expansion, and turnaround situations.

Michigan

Michigan Business Ombudsman

Michigan Department of Commerce
Michigan Business PO Box 30107
Lansing, MI 48909

Lansing, MI 48909

(517) 373-6241

(Toll-free number in Michigan: 1-800-232-2727)

This organization simplifies communications with the government. They do provide a one-stop source for permits and licensing information. They also have information on how to start a business in Michigan.

Small Business Centers

Local Development Services Bureau PO Box 30225

Lansing, MI 48909

(517)-373-3530

To find out which SBC is closest to you, contact the above address. The SBC provides personal assistance and counseling services in many different areas of business, these include, license and permit information, business procurement and export development, capital acquisition, financial packaging, plus additional state and local resources available in Michigan.

Division of Minority Business Enterprise

Michigan Department of Commerce

Michigan Business PO Box 30225

Lansing, MI 48909

(517)-373-8430

Provides assistance with training, education, management, and financial packaging.

Office Of Women Business Owners

Michigan Department of Commerce

Michigan Business PO Box 30225

Lansing, MI 48909

(517)-373-6224

Provides assistance with training, education, management, and financial packaging.

Minnesota

Small Business Development Centers
University of Minnesota
Agricultural Extension Service, Small Business Development Center
Department of Agriculture and Applied Economics
248 Classroom Building
St. Paul MN 55108
(612) 223-8663

Counseling, information assistance, and training are provided to beginning entrepreneurs or other small business owners in Minnesota. These centers are located throughout the state; contact the university to obtain the location nearest you.

Small Business Institutes
Bethel College, Small Business Institute
PO Box 77,
3900 Bethel Drive,
St. Paul MN 55112
(612) 638-6318

Students of the college under faculty supervision provide help for local businesses in the form of counseling and market information. The services are provided free, at various locations throughout the state.

Small Business Assistance Offices
Small Business Assistance Office
Minnesota Department of Energy and Economic Development
900 American Center Building
150 East Kellogg Boulevard,
St. Paul, MN 55107
(612) 296-3871

These centers provide direct assistance in helping new businesses to get on their feet. Financial assistance as well as counseling and management training are available. The offices are distributed throughout the state; the address above will be able to provide more information about regional offices.

Minnesota Trade Office
90 West Plato Boulevard,
St. Paul, MN 55107
(612) 297-4222

This office was set up to help state businesses (small to medium scale) to develop an export industry. Financial aid is offered under guidelines set up by the office. Also available is a research library to help business owners learn about market conditions overseas. Seminars are also provided.

Office of Project Management
Office of Project Management,
Minnesota Department of Energy and Economic Development
900 American Center Building
150 Kellogg Boulevard
St. Paul MN 55101
(612) 296-5005

This office provides information on obtaining financial assistance for businesses in Minnesota. Leads to sources of funding, as well as other monetary information is provided.

Minnesota Small Business Development Loans
Minnesota Department of Energy and Economic Development
900 American Center
150 East Kellogg Boulevard,
St. Paul MN 55101
(612) 296-6424

Loans ranging from $250,000 to $1 million in order to help struggling businesses are offered. Interest rates are below that paid by the government on its own loans. Up to 20 years financing is available.

The Minnesota Fund
Minnesota Department of Energy and Economic Development
900 American Center
150 East Kellogg Boulevard,
St. Paul MN 55101
(612) 296-7145

This program also offers loans for businesses in the state of Minnesota. Loans are made at fixed interest, have a ceiling of $250,000 and cannot exceed 20 percent of the total cost of the project.

Mississippi

Mississippi Research and Development Centers
Mississippi Research and Development Center
3825 Ridgewood Road
Jackson, MS 39211
(601) 982-6684

Beginning entrepreneurs seeking to establish a business in the state of Mississippi can receive free information from these centers. Help is in the form of limited counseling, seminars, and workshops. Assistance is also provided for those wishing to expand their already existing business.

Start-Up Training Program for Industry
Coordinator of Industry Services
Vocational-Technical Division
Mississippi State Department of Education, PO Box 771,
Jackson, MS 39205
(601) 359-3074

This program provides training for managerial and newer staff, and assists the company in writing a training outline. Also helps screen incoming employees to the business, or helps the company develop its own screening procedures.

Mississippi Department of Economic Development
Mississippi Department of Economic Development
PO Box 849,
Jackson MS 39205
(601) 359-3437

Guaranteed loans of up to $200,000; participates in the SBA (Small Business Administration) Guaranteed loan program with a maximum guarantee of $500,000. Also guarantees Industrial Revenue bonds of up to $10 million.

Missouri

Greater Kansas City Chamber of Commerce
Greater Kansas City Chamber of Commerce
Ten Main Center, Sixth Floor
920 Main St.
Kansas City, MO 64106

Counseling, seminars, and other informational services are offered.

One-Stop Shop
Missouri Division of Community and Economic Development
PO Box 118
Jefferson City, MO 65102
(314) 751-4982

Provides all necessary legal advice for starting a business in Missouri. Also publishes a booklet known as "Starting a New Business in Missouri" to help beginning entrepreneurs.

Business and Industry Extension Offices
Business and Industry Extension Office
1601 East 18th Street, Suite 200
Kansas City, MO 64108
(816) 472-0227

These offices provide counseling to new and established businesses in the state of Missouri. Services are free.

Business Resource Center
Business Resource Center
1139 Olive, Room 500,
St. Louis, MO 63101
(314) 621-7410

These centers provide a variety of business services free to members of minority groups.

Is Your Business At A Crossroads?

Need Directions?

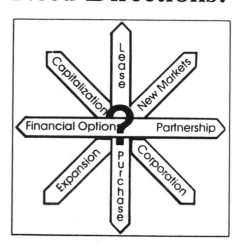

**TENNESSEE
SMALL BUSINESS
DEVELOPMENT CENTER
CONSULTANTS
CAN ASSIST YOU
AT NO COST**

Missouri Customized Training Program

Skills for Tomorrow's Work Force.

Black Economic Union
Black Economic Union
1710 Paseo,
Kansas City, MO 64127
(816) 474-1080

Provides counseling services and referrals for minority business owners.

Employee Training Funds
Missouri Customized Training Program
221 Metro Drive
Jefferson City, MO 65101
(314) 751-2372

This program provides funds to businesses for employee training, and also helps the business develop a training program. Half the wages of the employees to be trained are covered by the program.

Missouri Time Deposits for Industrial Development
Office of the State Treasurer
PO Box 210
Jefferson City MO 65105
(314) 751-2372

Loans are provided, in conjunction with local banks, to businesses recently locating or expanding their facilities in the state of Missouri.

Montana

Business Assistance Division
Business Assistance Division
Montana Department of Commerce
1424 Ninth Avenue,
Helena, MT 59620
(406) 444-3923

Provides counseling, information on procurement, export assistance, and other services.

University Center for Business and Management Development

University Center for Business and Management Development
445 Reid Hall
Montana State University
Bozeman, MT 59717
(406) 994-2057

Research assistance relating to market conditions is provided through this program, as well as help with training and other technical assistance. Offices are located throughout the state, contact the address above for the location nearest you.

Business Development Assistance

Business Assistance Division
Montana Department of Commerce
1424 Ninth Avenue
Helena, MT 59620
(406) 444-4325

Offers help with a variety of technical matters pertaining to business. These include obtaining financial aid, marketing, hiring, training, and quality control, among others.

US Government Procurement Assistance

Business Assistance Division,
Montana Department of Commerce
1424 Ninth Avenue
Helena, MT 59620
(406) 444-4325

This program assists small companies in all aspects of doing business with the government as well as with other businesses. Provides information on local opportunities, in one-to-one counseling.

Development Finance Technical Assistance

Business Assistance Division,
Montana Department of Commerce
Helena, MT 59620
(406) 444-4325

A collection of financial aid programs designed to encourage small business growth in Montana. Most financial aid is in the form of loans made at fixed rates and offered through commercial banks.

Montana Capital Companies
Montana Economic Development Board,
1424 Ninth Avenue,
Helena, MT 59620
(406) 444-2090

This program works to increase venture capital investment in small business in Montana. The state offers up to $25,000 in tax incentives to venture capital firms which agree to finance small businesses in Montana.

GUIDE TO BUSINESS ASSISTANCE PROGRAMS

MONTANA DEPARTMENT OF COMMERCE

JUNE 1989

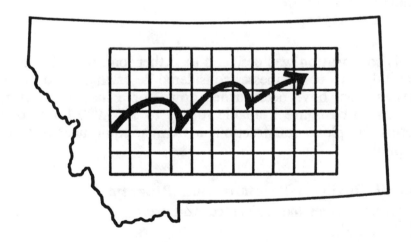

Nebraska

Nebraska Department of Economic Development

Nebraska Department of Economic Development
Small Business Division
Box 94666
301 Centennial Mall, South
Lincoln, NE 68509-4666
(402) 471-3111

The Small Business Division, works in conjunction with higher education business development centers in an effort to provide development of business plans, market planning, entrepreneurial identification, and management assistance. Offered as well is direct technical assistance in finance packaging, job training, procurement assistance, export promotion, and opportunity identification.

Business Development Corporation of Nebraska

Business Development Corporation of Nebraska
1044 Stuart Building
Lincoln, NE 68508
(402) 474-3855

This corporation was designed to gather loan funds for long-term capital loans to businesses considered deserving. Also, these businesses must have been turned down for a loan by conventional banks. Loans are available for up to $250,000 for 5-to-15-year terms for plant construction, materials, equipment and working capital.

Small Business Revitalization Program

Nebraska Investment Finance Authority
Gold's Galleria
Suite 304
1033 O Street
Lincoln, NE 68508
(402) 477-4406

Although this program does not have funds to loan, the SBRP will assist in putting together a financial package, at no cost to the business.

Nebraska Business Development Centers

Nebraska Business Development Center
College of Business Administration
University of Nebraska at Omaha
Omaha, NE 68182
(402) 554-2521

The types of programs the NBDC offers include: business and financial analysis, individual management consultations, feasibility studies, workshops and seminars, monthly business reports, special studies, new business counseling, capital formation and market research assistance.

Nebraska Technical Assistance Center

Nebraska Technical Assistance Center
W191 Nebraska Hall
University of Nebraska-Lincoln
Lincoln, NE 68588-0535
(402) 472-5600
Toll-free Nebraska number: 800 742-8800

These programs will provide consultants for diagnostic assistance, as well as supplying engineering professionals to Nebraska manufacturers. Workshops and seminars are also included, as well as information on marketing and financial assistance.

U.S. Small Business Administration

U.S. Small Business Administration
Management Assistance
Empire State Building
Nineteenth and Farnam Streets
Omaha, NE 68102
(402) 221-3604

This agency provides information on procuring contracts with the federal government. The Procurement Automated Source System (PASS) has a complete list of businesses which have the capabilities of fitting government or contractors needs.

Small Business Administration, 503 Loan

Business Development Corporation of Nebraska
1044 Stuart Building
Lincoln, NE 68508

(402) 474-3855

Through this program, lenders provide small business customers with low-interest, long-term, fixed asset financing. **There are three sources for the SBA 503 package:** 1) the Small Business Administration, 2) private lending institutions, 3) the small business concern. The private lending institution will provide up to 50 percent of the total project cost at conventional interest rates. Up to 40 percent of the project cost is provided by the SBA. This will not exceed $500,000 at an interest rate of approximately 3/4 percent above long-term US Treasury Bond rates. The small business concern is responsible for the remaining balance.

Nebraska Investment Finance Authority

Nebraska Investment Finance Authority
Gold's Galleria
Suite 304
1033 O Street
Lincoln, NE 68508
(402) 477-4406

This agency will provide low-cost financing for agricultural, industrial, health care and residential development. Low-cost funds are furnished by the Business Development Loan Program for the purchase of equipment for businesses in Nebraska. The NIFA will work with lending sources throughout the state, to insure below-market, fixed interest rates to eligible borrowers. NIFA will back a maximum loan of $850,000 and a minimum of $40,000. The depreciation of the business equipment will have a bearing on the terms of the loan (under federal tax codes), with seven years being the maximum loan time.

Industrial Development Revenue Bonds

Nebraska Department of Economic Development
P.O. Box 94666
301 Centennial Mall South
Lincoln, NE 68509
(402) 471-3111

Through tax-exempt bond issues, low-cost financing is provided to eligible projects. These bonds can be authorized by counties and municipalities. Those projects deemed eligible must be of an industrial nature. Interest rates on the bonds are determined on the company's credit, and since the interest is tax-exempt, the rates will be lower than those of a conventional lending institution.

Community Development Block Grant
Division of Community Affairs
Nebraska Department of Economic Development
P.O. Box 94666
301 Centennial Mall South
Lincoln, NE 68509
(402) 471-3111

The premise of this program is to supplement other sources of finance in order to direct funds toward local economic development issues. The funded projects must also address the creation of jobs for low-to moderate income residents.

Nevada

Nevada Commission on Economic Development
Nevada Commission on Economic Development
Capitol Complex
Carson City, NV 89710
(702) 885-4325

This program will provide information concerning land availability, feasibility studies, industrial parks, economic development districts, and educational and training programs.

Nevada Small Business Development Centers
Nevada Small Business Development Center
College of Business Administration
University of Nevada-Reno
Business Building
Room 411
Reno, NV 89557-0016
(702) 784-1717

This program offers management assistance at no cost to small businesses in Nevada. Included in the counseling is market research assistance, marketing strategies, business workshops, feasibility studies, capital formation assistance, as well as other counseling programs.

Business Development Council

Business Development Council
Greater Reno-Sparks Chamber of Commerce
133 North Sierra Street
Reno, NV 89501
(702) 786-3030

Through this program planning and counseling services are offered to small businesses providing the majority of goods and services to a particular area.

Training and Consultation Section (TACS)

Division of Occupational Safety and Health
1370 South Curry Street
Carson City, NV 89710
(702) 885-5240

Designed to assist employers in protecting their employees against work-related injuries and health hazards. Consultations may include both the employer and the employees. No compliance inspections will be conducted during the TAC visit, so employers do not have to worry about being cited for safety or health violations that may be noticed.

Industrial Development Revenue Bonds

Nevada Department of Commerce
201 South Fall Street
Carson City, NV 89710
(702) 885-4340

This program will provide up to 100 percent financing for land, building, capital equipments and improvements specifically for businesses incurring $1 to $10 million in developing costs. Applicants must meet state eligibility requirements.

Nevada Small Business Revitalization Program

Nevada Small Business Revitalization Program
Community Services Office
1100 East Williams
Suite 117
Carson City, NV 89710
(702) 885-4420

Financial assistance, sponsored by the SBA and HUD grant monies, is given to small businesses for economic development planning.

Northern Nevada Job Training Program

Northern Nevada Job Training Program
120 South Wells
Reno, NV 89502
(702) 885-8353
Toll-free number in Nevada: 800 648-0599

In order to reduce the cost of training new employees an On-the-Job Training Program has been implemented by the state of Nevada. Job applicants (although hired on a permanent basis and by the employer) are put on a three month probationary period, wherein that time, if the occupation is learned effectively, they are retained by the employer. The state will then reimburse the employer for up to 50 percent of the cost to train the employee. All applicants are prescreened.

Reno-Sparks Chamber of Commerce

Reno-Sparks Chamber of Commerce
133 North Sierra Street
Reno, NV 89501
(702) 885-4420

Holds monthly events to encourage small owners and the public to interact. Also provides business counseling for these businesses and publishes a business source guide.

Nevada Revolving Loan Program

Nevada Small Business Revitalization Program
Commission on Economic Development
Capital Complex
Carson City, NV 89710
(702) 687-4325

This program was created for small business expansion and to furnish employment opportunities for low-to-moderate income persons. The program will loan up to 40 percent, or $100,000, depending on which is the lesser of the total project cost. The bank will finance the remaining 60 percent. Second trust deed on the project property is usually the loan collateral.

New Hampshire

Small Business Development Center
Small Business Development Center
New Hampshire Small Business Program
400 Commercial St.
Room 311
Manchester, NH 03101
(603) 862-3556
Toll-free number in New Hampshire: 800 332-0390

This program, (offered to entrepreneurs and existing firms) offers management counseling and education and information referral. Consulting covers such areas as marketing, loan packaging, production control and financial analysis. These services are offered at no charge.

Venture Capital Network
New Hampshire Small Business Program
Kingman Farm
University of New Hampshire
Durham, NH 03824
(603) 862-3556

An organized network that puts together businesspersons seeking financial backing from venture capitalists.

New Hampshire Business Development Corporation
New Hampshire Business Development Corporation
P.O. Box 1109
Concord, NH 03302
(603) 224-1432

Through this program, businesses which are deemed promising will be awarded a line of credit which they would otherwise not be able to secure. Interest rates are negotiable.

Technical Assistance Program
New Hampshire Small Business Program
110 McConnell Hall
Durham, NH 03824

UNIVERSITY OF NEW HAMPSHIRE

Equity Financing for New Technology-Based Firms

COMPLIMENTARY

Center for Venture Research

Affiliated with the Whittemore School of Business & Economics
University of New Hampshire
Durham, New Hampshire 03824

Delaware Small Business Development Center

•

Management Counseling

•

Business Training

•

Business Information

•

(603)862-3556
Marketing and technical assistance in selected sections of New Hampshire.

Granite State Capital, Incorporated

Granite State Capital, Inc.
10 Fort Eddy Road
Concord, NH 03301
(603) 228-9090

Assists talented entrepreneurs in acquiring equity capital and constructive counsel to build a substantial business.

The University of New Hampshire Consulting Center

Consulting Center
Research Office
Horton Social Science Center
University of New Hampshire
Durham, NH 03824
(603) 862-3750

The center will assist with product development, technical trouble shooting, risk analysis and planning, software development, market analysis, long-range research and planning, as well as other related topics.

Business Assistance for Northern New Hampshire

New Hampshire Small Business Program
400 Commercial St.
Room 311
Manchester, NH 03101
(603) 862-3556

Program to support new and growing companies by providing direct technical and managerial assistance. Also, this program will link private businesses with private and public organizations which offers support services.

New Hampshire Industrial Development Revenue Bond Financing

Industrial Development Authority
Four Park Street
Room 302
Concord, NH 03301

(603) 271-2391

Credit-worthy companies can receive tax-exempt revenue bond financing at an interest rate that is far below normal conventional rates.

Northern Community Investment Corporation
Northern Community Investment Corporation
P.O. Box 188
Littlejohn, NH 03561
(603) 298-5546

This program will provide to commercial, residential, and industrial properties, loan guarantees, direct loans, and financial and technical development for Carroll, Grafton, and Coos Counties. NCIC financing is available.

New Jersey

Office of Minority Business Enterprise
Office of Minority Business Enterprise
New Jersey Department of Commerce
and Economic Development
Division of Administration
CN 990
Trenton, NJ 08625
(609) 292-1800

Assistance is offered to minority-owned businesses in regard to bidding on state procurement contracts.

Office of Small Business Assistance
Office of Small Business Assistance
New Jersey Department of Commerce
and Economic Development
1 West State Street
CN 823
Trenton, NJ 08625
(609) 984-4442

Program to assist entrepreneurs in starting up a new business.

NEW JERSEY
HAS AN
OFFICE OF
WOMEN BUSINESS ENTERPRISE

Division of Development for Small Businesses
and Women and Minority Businesses
**New Jersey Department of Commerce, Energy
and Economic Development**
20 West State Street, CN 835
Trenton, NJ 08625-0835

BROWN VENTURE FORUM

THE ENTREPRENEUR'S

RESOURCE GUIDE

*A listing of resources committed to fostering the formation and growth
of new businesses.*

*Compiled by the Brown University Research Foundation,
Box 1949, Providence, RI 02912
401-863-3528*

Corporation for Business Assistance in New Jersey

Corporation for Business Assistance in New Jersey
200 South Warren Street
Suite 600
Trenton, NJ 08608
(609) 633-7737

This program provides small businesses with up to 25 years of fixed asset financing. This is for the acquisition of land, machinery, construction, and restoration.

New Jersey Economic Development Authority

New Jersey Economic Development Authority
Capital Place One
CN 990
Trenton, NJ 08625
(609) 292-1800

Low-interest, long-term financing is arranged for expanding businesses in the New Jersey area. Programs include: Loan Guarantees and Direct Loans, SBA 503 Loan Program, Tax-exempt Industrial Bond Financing, and Local Development Financing Fund Loans.

New Mexico

Industrial Site Location Assistance

New Mexico Economic Development and Tourism Dept.
Bataan Memorial Building
Room 201 EDB
Santa Fe, NM 87503
(505) 827-6200

Assistance from professional economic and/or industrial developer for companies trying to locate a business site.

Development Training Programs

New Mexico Economic Development and Tourism Dept.
Bataan Memorial Building
Room 201 EDB
Santa Fe, NM 87503
(505) 827-6200

This program provides state sponsored funds to train workers in the New Mexico area. The state will pay one-half of the wages of the trainee during the training period.

New Mexico Economic Development and Tourism Dept.
New Mexico Economic Development and Tourism Dept.
Bataan Memorial Building
Room 201 EDB
Santa Fe, NM 87503
(505) 827-6200

Information and assistance in obtaining low-interest, long- term loans. Sources of financial assistance include: SBA 503 Guaranteed Loan, Community Development Block Grant, Industrial Revenue Bonds, Economic Incentive Loan Program, Industrial and Agricultural Finance Authority, and Business Development Corporation.

New York

Office of Business Permits
Office of Business Permits
Alfred E. Smith State Office Building
Albany, NY 12225
(518) 474-8275
Toll-free number in New York: 800 342-3464

Offers information and assistance and issues business permits for businesses in New York.

Minority and Women's Business Division
Minority and Women's Business Division
230 Park Avenue
Suite 1825
New York, NY 10169
(212) 309-0440

This program provides business planning and financial packaging assistance through a bilingual staff. Regularly scheduled meetings are held in order to assist female minority business owners in the state of New York.

New York Business Development Corporation

New York Business Development Corporation
41 State Street
Albany, NY 12207
(518) 463-2268

It loans funds to undercapitalized firms when other sources of financial assistance can not be obtained from conventional sources.

Urban Development Corporation

Urban Development Corporation
1515 Broadway
New York, NY 10036
(212) 930-9000

Program which provides financial assistance to minority businesswomen who own their own businesses.

New York Job Development Authority

New York Job Development Authority
One Commerce Plaza
Albany, NY 12210
(518) 474-7580

Works as a bank in the respect of providing business and industrial loans for real estate and work related equipment.

Small Business Division Assistance Program

New York Department of Commerce
Division for Small Business
230 Park Avenue
New York, NY 10169
(212) 309-0400

This program was designed to assist small businesses in getting started or expanding their operation. The programs include: Small Business Counseling, Small Business Task Force, Training and Technical Assistance, State Training and Manpower Program (STAMP), Procurement Assistant, NYS Small Business Advisory Board, and Business Services Ombudsman.

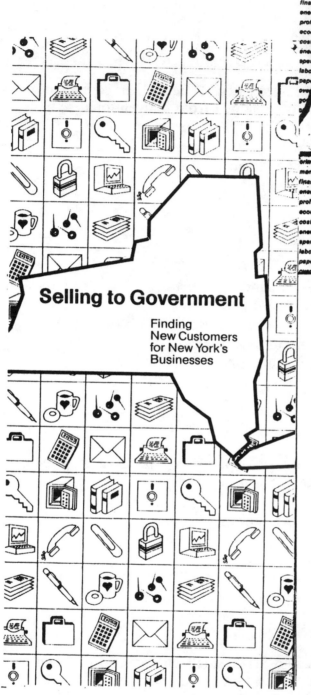

CUTTING GOVERNMENT RED-TAPE FOR NEW YORK'S BUSINESSES

Selling to Government

Finding New Customers for New York's Businesses

New York State

Small Business Advisory Board

INFORMATION BULLETIN

MINORITY AND WOMEN REVOLVING LOAN FUND

STATE OF NEW YORK

MARIO M. CUOMO
GOVERNOR

VINCENT TESE
CHAIRMAN

 New York State Urban Development Corporation

North Carolina

North Carolina Department of Commerce
Business Assistance Division
Department of Commerce
430 North Salisbury Street
Raleigh, NC 27611
(919) 733-7980

The state of North Carolina has no loans available to small businesses although there are several business counseling and informational programs which can assist with choosing the proper Small Business Administration program.

North Carolina Small Business and
Technology Development Center
North Carolina SBTDC
820 Clay Street
Raleigh, NC 27605
(919) 733-4643

Business counseling and information is provided by university faculty and graduate students. Service is provided free of charge.

Small Business Institute
Small Business Institute
Department of Business Administration
UNCC
Charlotte, NC 28223
(704) 597-4424
Provides free business counseling through graduate/senior student and faculty advisory teams.

Minority Business Assistance
North Carolina State MBDA
Department of Commerce
430 North Salisbury Street
Raleigh, NC 27611
(919) 597-4424

Counseling and business information provided to minorities, women, and socially disadvantaged individuals.

Small Business Resource Centers
Greater Charlotte Chamber of Commerce
129 West Trade Street
P.O. Box 32785
Charlotte, NC 28232
(704) 377-6911

Provides information on small business management, training, and other services offered by the Small Business Administration.

North Dakota

Small Business Institute
Small Business Institute
Business Administration and Economics
North Dakota State University
Putnam Hall
Fargo, ND 58105
(701) 237-7690
Through this program, North Dakota State University graduate students and faculty provide business counseling and information to small business.

North Dakota Economic Development Commission
North Dakota Economic Development Commission
Liberty Memorial Building
Bismarck, ND 58501
(701) 224-2810
Toll-free number in North Dakota: 800 472-2100

Program which guides new or expanding businesses in regard to their finances. When appropriate, the commission works as a mediator with the financier.

Center for Innovation and Business Development
Center for Innovation and
Business Development
Box 8103
University Station
Grand Forks, ND 58202
(701) 777-3132

Provides information and counseling for technical development, invention evaluation, and business development.

Ohio

Small Business Enterprise Centers
Small Business Enterprise Center Office
Ohio Department of Development
P.O. Box 1001
Columbus, OH 43266
(614) 466-5700

This program provides counseling services and information for small businesses regarding: technical resources, funding sources, educational programs, procurement assistance, legal assistance, and management and technical assistance.

Women's Business Resource Program
Women's Business Resource Program
Small and Developing Business Division
Ohio Department of Development
P.O. Box 1001
Columbus, OH 43266-0101
(614) 466-2115

This program assists women who own businesses with the loan packaging, purchasing, and the procurement opportunities with government agencies and private industries. Also offers workshops and seminars.

Business Development Services
Business Development Division
Ohio Department of Development
P.O. Box 1001
Columbus, OH 43266
(614) 466-2317
Toll-free in Ohio: 800 282-1085

Offers relocation and site selection services for small businesses.

**Center for
Innovation &
Business
Development**

Box 8103, University Station
Grand Forks, North Dakota 58202
Phone: (701) 777-3132 Fax: (701) 777-5181

"HOMEGROWN" MANUFACTURING

New Business Through Innovation

The Center for Innovation and Business Development provides business and technical support services to entrepreneurs, inventors, and small manufacturers. The emphasis is on new product development, manufacturing start-ups, and technology transfer, creating new jobs and new wealth by helping creative individuals reach their innovative potential.

<u>Idea Evaluation Services</u> - An evaluation service designed to determine the commercial and technical viability of an idea, invention, or new product. Honest, objective evaluation should precede further development of any idea, and may save the inventor and entrepreneur considerable resources and time.

- o Invention Evaluation Service - Preliminary commercial evaluation
- o **Energy Related Inventions Program** - Technical evaluation and grants
  for further development upon favorable review (up to $200,000 in grants)
- o Market Feasibility Studies and Competitive Analysis
- o Assistance with patent searches, patents, trademarks, and copyrights

<u>Business Plan Preparation and Review</u> - A business plan is vital for management planning, and for attracting debt and equity financing. Good ideas with a comprehensive business plan will attract the required resources for successful development. The Center is receiving national attention for their business plan services and publications, especially for manufacturing start-ups with new products.

- o Business Plan Book and Software - step-by-step self-help guides
- o Assistance in writing the plan utilizing staff, students, faculty, and consultants
- o Review and analysis of business plans for entrepreneurs, banks, and
  professionals in economic development
- o Financial analysis with a comparison to industry standards

<u>Debt and Equity Financing</u> - Prepares entrepreneurs to approach sources of debt and equity financing, including preparing the finance package. Several of our clients have raised over a million dollars in financing with our assistance.

- o Working with federal, state, and local sources of debt financing
- o Associated with several venture capitalists around the nation
- o Work with the North Dakota Venture Capital Corporation (Myron Nelson Fund)
- o Administer the First Seed Capital Group, (investors in private companies
  from around North Dakota)

<u>Research Technology Transfer</u> - Assistance in the commercialization of new knowledge from university research and other sources. There are many commercially viable ideas without an entrepreneur, and bringing the vital components together will expand existing companies launch new ventures.

- o SBIR grants which provide small companies with up to $50,000 for feasibility
  studies, and up to $500,000 for R & D
- o Assistance with writing grant applications

—————— The University of North Dakota ——————
School of Engineering & Mines Foundation

Technology Information Exchange-Innovation Network (Tie-In)
Division of Technological Innovation
Department of Development
30 East Broad Street
P.O. Box 1001
Columbus, OH 43266
(614) 466-3086

Provides assistance with the start up and development of small businesses.

One-Stop Business Permit Center
One-Stop Business Permit Center
30 East Broad Street
Columbus, OH 43216
(614) 462-8748

Will assist businesses with information for obtaining necessary business permits.

Economic Development Financing Division
Economic Development Financing Division
Ohio Department of Development
P.O. Box 1001
Columbus, OH 43266
(614) 466-5420

Program that offers loan guarantees, direct loans, and industrial and hospital revenue bonds.

Oklahoma

Small Business Development Centers
Small Business Development Center
East Central University
1036 East 10th Street
Ada, OK 74820
(405) 436-3190

This program provides free assistance to small businesspersons for the reason of starting or expanding a business already in existence.

Oklahoma Industrial Finance Authority
Oklahoma Industrial Finance Authority
4024 Lincoln Boulevard
Oklahoma City, OK 73105
(405) 521-2182

This program provides industries involved with manufacturing with supplemental loan packages of up to 25 percent for the acquisition of land, machinery, and buildings.

Venture Capital Exchange
Venture Capital Exchange
Enterprise Development Center
The University of Tulsa
600 South College Avenue
Tulsa, OK 74104
(918) 592-6000 Ext. 3152 or 2684

Brings together entrepreneurs and venture capitalists. This service involves a $100 fee for every entrepreneur-opportunity application, but is good for one year.

Oregon

Economic Development Department
Economic Development Department
595 Cottage Street, N.E.
Salem, OR 97310
(503) 373-1200

Assistance to obtain state and federal loans including: Oregon Resource and Technology Development Corporation, Small Business Administration 503 Loan Program, Umbrella Revenue Bond, Oregon Business Development Fund, Port Revolving Loan Fund, and Urban Development Action Grant.

Business Development Division
Business Development Division
595 Cottage Street, N.E.
Salem, OR 97310
(503) 373-1200

Oregon business are eligible to receive a variety of management services.

Small Business Development Centers

Small Business Development Center
OSBDCN State Offices
Lane Community College
1059 Willamette Street
Eugene, OR 97401
(503) 373-1225

This program offers services to small businesses which include business counseling and training, as well as information and resources at little or no cost.

"One-Stop" Permit Information Office

"One-Stop" Permit Information Office
595 Cottage Street, N.E.
Salem, OR 97310
(503) 373-1234

This office gives information and assistance in regard to necessary permits required in Oregon.

Pennsylvania

Small Business Action Center

Small Business Action Center
P.O. Box 8100
Harrisburg, PA 17105
(717) 783-5700

This center will provide the Pennsylvania businessman/woman with information regarding government regulations and taxes affecting their businesses, as well as supplying all necessary business forms. This center keeps all these forms on hand, so you don't have to call all over town trying to locate what you need. This center also keeps information regarding available federal, state, local and private funding sources. Also available through this center are business counseling and managerial assistance.

Pennsylvania Industrial Development Authority (PIDA)
Pennsylvania Department of Commerce
Bureau of Economic Assistance, PIDA
405 Forum Building
Harrisburg, PA 17120
(717) 787-6245

This agency awards low-interest loans to businesses located in areas with a high unemployment rate, to induce economic movement. These loans are used for new construction, renovations, expansion of already existing buildings, and land and building acquisitions. Up to 70 percent financing is available to eligible projects.

Pennsylvania Capital Loan Fund Program
Pennsylvania Department of Commerce
Bureau of Economic Assistance
405 Forum Building
Harrisburg, PA 17120
(717) 783-1768

This program awards eligible businesses with low-interest loans for capital development projects in order to stimulate employment opportunities. These loans are used for building and land acquisition, renovations, and the purchase of work related equipment. Up to $50,000 or 20 percent of the total project cost may be awarded to eligible businesses.

Small Business Development Centers
State Director's Office
Wharton School
Small Business Development Center
343 Vance Hall/CS
Philadelphia, PA 19104
(215) 898-1219

These centers offer managerial assistance and business counseling to small businesses. Other services include market research, financial analysis, accounting assistance and business planning. While most of the services are free, others may charge a small fee. The centers are located in various colleges throughout the state.

Pennsylvania Technical Assistance Program (PENNTAP)
Pennsylvania State University
Capital Campus
Small Business Development Center
Crags Building
Route 230
Middletown, PA 17057
(717) 948-6031

This program brings together those businesses which are having technical problems with industries which can provide them with solutions. Full-time service technicians offer assistance with production, product development, energy sources and computerized systems. PENNTAP does not charge for these services.

Industrial Revenue Bonds
Revenue Bond & Mortgage Program
Pennsylvania Department of Commerce
Bureau of Economic Assistance
405 Forum Building
Harrisburg, PA 17120
(717) 783-1108

This program provides tax-exempt financing for the purpose of land acquisition, buildings, and equipment for industrial and commercial businesses. Bond maturity can range from 10 to 35 years, and loans range from 10 to 20 years. Refinancing with these funds is not permitted.

Pennsylvania Minority Business Development Authority
Headquarters/Central Region
406 South Office Building
Harrisburg, PA 17120
(717) 783-1127

This program provides minority owned businesses that wish to expand, with low-interest, long-term loans. It also provides funds for disadvantaged businesses that can not obtain an additional conventional loan. Loan rates are approximately one-half of the prime rate. Assistance offered includes technical, management, financial planning and accounting assistance and marketing strategies.

Employee Ownership Assistance Program
Pennsylvania Department of Commerce
405 Forum Building
Harrisburg, PA 17120
(717) 783-6890

This program will provide low-interest loans to employees who are interested in ownership of the firm they are working for. This money will cover the costs of feasibility studies, technical assistance, land acquisition or rehabilitation, and working capital. Up to $100,000 or 50 percent (whichever is less) is available for feasibility studies and technical services. Studies must be concluded within one year of the issuance of the loan. Loan terms can not exceed 20 years.

Rhode Island

Rhode Island Department of Economic Development

Rhode Island Department of Economic Development
7 Jackson Walkway
Providence, RI 02903
Phone: (401) 277-2601
Description: Provides information about state and local business problems. Also provides counseling, export assistance, federal procurement assistance, research and marketing, and site selection assistance.

Rhode Island Small Business Development Centers

Rhode Island Small Business Development Center
Bryant College
Smithfield, RI 02917
Phone: (401) 232-6111
Description: Provides person-to-person consultation services to existing and start-up small businesses. Runs seminars and training programs. Maintains a staff of professional consultants in a variety of financial management and marketing specialties.

Brown Venture Forum

Brown Venture Forum
Box 1949
Providence, RI 02912
Phone: (401) 863-3528
Description: Provides a forum for entrepreneurs, venture capitalists, experienced business executives, and others who share the goal of starting and expanding businesses. Free open meetings are held each month and sponsors start-up clinics and workshops.

Rhode Island Department of Economic Development

Rhode Island Department of Economic Development
7 Jackson Parkway
Providence, RI 02903
Phone: (401) 277-2601
Description: Gives information on the many financial assistance programs available to help new and expanding businesses, including Industrial Revenue Bonds, Insured Mortgage Financing, Revolving Loan Funds, and Business Investment Funds.

South Carolina

Small Business Development Centers

Small Business Development Center
College of Business Administration
University of South Carolina
Columbia, SC 29208
Phone: (803) 777-5118

Description: Provides free information and assistance to small businesses that are or are soon to be expanding. One-on-one consultation is available.

Customized Industrial Training

Division of Industrial and Economic Development
South Carolina State Board for Technical and Comprehensive Education
111 Executive Center Drive
Columbia, SC 29210
Phone: (803) 758-6926

Description: Provides pre-employment and on-the-job training to meet the needs of new and expanding manufacturers. Training is normally conducted prior to employment. Trainees are not paid for the time spent in training.

South Carolina State Development Board

South Carolina State Development Board
PO Box 927
Columbia, SC 29202
Phone: (803) 758-3046

Description: Distributes Industrial Revenues Bonds to enterprises engaged in: Dealing with products of agriculture, mining or industry; manufacturing or growing, processing or assembling, storage, warehousing, distributing, and selling; and research in connection with any of these. The maximum term of individual bond issues is 40 years, although in practice, terms range from 10 to 25 years depending on the money market. There is no limit on interest rates, which can be negotiated between the bond purchaser and the company using the facility.

South Carolina Jobs - Economic Development Authority Pooled Investment Program

Jobs-Economic Development Authority
Number One Main Building
1203 Gervais Street

Columbia, SC 29201

Phone: (803) 758-2094

Description: Obtains low-cost funds, both variable and fixed rate, for small businesses through the sale of tax-exempt industrial revenue bonds. The ceiling amount available to a single enterprise is $10 million and the minimum loan given is $100,000. The term of the bonds issued is determined by the local bank issuing the credit.

Jobs-Economic Development Authority

Jobs-Economic Development Authority

1203 Gervais Street

Columbia, SC 29201

Phone: (803) 758-2094

Description: Direct state loans are available to assist private enterprises and are confined to manufacturing, industrial or service businesses. Funds may be used for land; construction, acquisition, or renovation of facilities; equipment; raw materials; and, in some locations, working capital. Loan rates vary from 85% of prime to prime rate plus 1%. Rate depends on terms of the average local prime rate of the major lending institutions, but not less than 8.5%. The rates are fixed and the loan amount cannot exceed $10,000 per new job created. The maximum funding amount is $250,000. Loan term cannot exceed 15 years.

Business Development Corporation of South Carolina

Business Development Corporation of South Carolina

Suite 225, Enoree Building

111 Executive Center Drive

Columbia, SC 29210

Phone: (803) 798-4064

Description: Provides financing to businesses unable to secure loans from conventional lending sources. BDCSC makes direct loans to businesses for new and expanding operations. The maximum loan term is 10 years. The corporation will borrow capital from member institutions at .5% above the prime rate and in turn charges a slightly higher rate on loans to businesses. The rate may be fixed or variable. Loan proceeds can be used for most business purposes, including fixed asset financing and working capital, providing the expenditure is related to creating or maintaining jobs.

South Dakota

Small Business Development Centers
Small Business Development Center
South Dakota Chamber of Commerce
PO Box 747
Rapid City, SD 57709
Phone: (605) 343-1744
Description: Provides free information and assistance to small businesspeople who wish to start or expand their business. One-on-one counseling is available.

State Development Office
South Dakota Department of State Development
Capitol Link Plaza
Box 6000
Pierre, SD 57501
Phone: 1-800-843-8000 (In South Dakota 800-952-3625)
Description: Assists new and expanding businesses to prepare packages to obtain private funding, industrial revenue bonds, SBA loans and even block grants.

Tennessee

Small Business Development Centers
The Fogelman College of Business Economics
Memphis State University
Memphis, TN 38152
Phone: (901) 454-2431

Description: These centers provide managerial and technical help, research studies and other types of specialized assistance of value to small businesses. These centers provide individual counseling and practical training for small business owners.

Small Business Institutes
Memphis State University
College of Business Administration
SBI Director
Memphis, TN 38152
Phone: (901) 454-2500

ECONOMIC DEVELOPMENT PROGRAMS

*South Dakota Programs Available to Assist
Businesses and Communities Help Themselves*

University of North Dakota

INVENTION EVALUATION SERVICE

*Providing an Opportunity for
Inventors to Gain Further
Insight into the Commercial
and Market Feasibility of
Their Innovations*

South Dakota

Governor's Office of Economic Development
Capitol Lake Plaza
Pierre, SD 57501
(605) 773-5032

Center for Innovation and
Business Development
Engineering Experiment Station
Box 8103, University Station
Grand Forks, North Dakota 58202
701-777-3132

Offices are located on campus at
212 Harrington Hall
College of Engineering

Description: Provides on-site management counseling through senior and graduate students at business administration schools.

Office of Minority Business Enterprise

Tennessee Department of Economic and Community Development
Office of Minority Business Enterprise
Room 1027, Andrew Jackson Building
Nashville, TN 37219
Phone: (615) 741-2546 (In Tennessee, 1-800-342-8470)
Description: Provides minority businesses with greater access to local economic planning data and resources of local governments, provides minority entrepreneurs with greater access to data concerning existing and emerging business trends and market conditions in Tennessee, provides assistance with loan packaging and preparation of business plans, and publishes a business newsletter for minority businesses in the state.

Office of Small Business

Tennessee Department of Economic and Community Development
Office of Small Business
Room 1025, Andrew Jackson Building
Nashville, TN 37219
Phone: (615) 741-5020 (In Tennessee, 1-800-342-8470)
Description: Information center for new small businesses in need of details on licences, permits, and taxes. Also assists small businesses in identifying procurement opportunities.

Department of Economic and Community Development

Tennessee Department of Economic and Community Development
Program Management Section, James K. Polk Building
Nashville, TN 37219
Phone: (615) 741-6201
Description: This department offers financing information for businesses in Tennessee. They can provide help with start-up financing or working capital in the form of loans or grants.

Texas

Regional Business Development Center

Texas Economic Development Commission,
410 East Fifth Street, PO Box 12728
Capitol Station, Austin TX 78711
Phone: (512) 472-5059
Description: Develops and promotes a healthy regional economy by sponsoring a variety of programs. These include financial assistance, market development programs, and information services. Help is provided to local businesses as well as to regional chambers of commerce.

Industrial Start-Up Training

Texas Economic Development Commission,
Industrial Locations and Services Department
PO Box 12728, Capitol Station,
Austin, TX 78711
Phone: (512) 472-5059
Description: Provides training of unskilled workers for industries planning to locate in Texas.

Business Regulations Assistance Center

Business Regulations Assistance Center
Texas Economic Development Commission,
PO Box 12728, Capitol Station
Austin, Texas 78711
Phone: (512) 472-5059
Description: This department provides information on taking a business public (incorporating), obtaining permits and licenses, and legal matters pertaining to state laws concerning businesses. Also provides methods to locate additional, more specialized information. Help is mostly given to new businesses, or those recently locating within the state.

Texas Economic Development Commission

Texas Economic Development Commission
410 East 5th Street, PO Box 12728
Capitol Station, Austin Texas 78711
Phone: (512) 472-5059
Description: Provides financial assistance for small businesses. Programs include Industrial Revenue Bonds, Small Business

Revitalization, and the Texas Small Business Industrial Development Corporation.

Utah

Small Business Development Centers

Small Business Development Center
660 South-200 East, Room 418
Salt Lake City, UT 84111
Phone: (801) 581-7905

Description: Assistance and information for businesspeople starting or expanding a small business. Individual consultation is available.

Davis County Economic Development Department

Davis County Economic Development Department
PO Box 305
Farmington, UT 84025
Phone: (801) 451-3264
Description: Business loans for land and building acquisition, building construction and renovation, machinery and equipment, and working capital. The maximum loan amount is 35% on loans up to $100,000. Term for capital assets is 5-20 years, for working capital, 3-7 years. Interest rates are negotiable.

Vermont

Small Business Development Centers

Small Business Development Centers
University of Vermont Extension Service
Morrill Hall
Burlington, VT 05405
Phone: (802) 656-4459
Description: Offers small business workshops, counseling, business planning, a comprehensive resource and information library, and a referral system linking other small business assistance organizations.

Vermont Industrial Development Authority

Vermont Industrial Development Authority
58 East Street
Montpelier, VT 05602
Phone: (802) 223-7226
Description: Offers low-interest loans to businesses for the purchase of land, purchase and construction of buildings, and purchase of equipment and machinery for use in an "industrial facility." Loans may be made for up to 30% of a project, with a local development corporation generally providing 10% of the costs and the balance being provided by an independent lending institution or government agency.

Small Business Revitalization Program

The Vermont Agency of Development and Community Affairs
109 State Street
Montpelier, VT 05602
Phone: (802) 828-3221 (In Vermont: 1-800-622-4553)

Description: Provides long-term financing through the utilization of a combination of federal, state and private sources of capital. The staff will review the borrower's needs and sort through the variety of public programs to recommend the best combination financing package to meet those needs.

Virginia

Office of Small Business and Financial Services

Office of Small Business and Financial Services
Virginia Department of Economic Development
1000 Washington Building
Richmond, VA 23219
Phone: (804) 786-3791
Description: Provides information on technical, management, and financial assistance programs operating throughout Virginia. A One-Stop Shop and Clearinghouse is available for prospective and established business owners, providing information on the various state agencies and business information.

Small Business Development Center

George Mason University Small Business Development Center
School of Business Administration, George Mason University
4400 University Drive
Fairfax, VA 22030
Phone: (703) 323-2568
Description: Provides special projects and financial facilitation; research, publications, and information; management training; technical assistance; and management counseling.

Virginia Business Opportunities

Virginia Business Opportunities
Virginia Department of General Services
Division of Purchases and Supply
PO Box 1199
Richmond, VA 23209
Phone: (804) 786-5494
Description: This publication is produced weekly and lists current business opportunities with the Commonwealth of Virginia. The cost is $60 a year.

Small Business Financing Authority

Small Business Financing Authority
1000 Washington Building
Richmond, VA 23219
Phone: (804) 786-3791
Description: The Umbrella Industrial Development Bond Program provides long-term financing of fixed assets to larger businesses.

Industrial Revenue Bonds

Division of Industrial Development, Community Development Division
1010 State Office Building
Richmond, VA 23219
Phone: (804) 371-8109
Description: Financing covers land, buildings, machinery, and equipment. Bonds provide up to 100% financing and permit an interest-cost savings over conventional financing owing to the tax-free interest received by investors who buy the bonds.

Local Development Corporations

Virginia Department of Economic Development
Office of Small Business and Financial Services

1000 Washington Building
Richmond, VA 23219
Phone: (804) 786-3791
Description: Many services are available, including: Direct loans to small businesses in their locations, site selection and assistance in applying for industrial revenue bonding, and Small Business Administration Loans.

Small Business Investment Companies
Virginia Department of Economic Development
Office of Small Business and Financial Services
1000 Washington Building
Richmond, VA 23219
Phone: (804) 786-3791
Description: Provides small businesses with equity capital and long-term loans. SBICs also offer management assistance to the companies they finance. The minimum financing term is 5 years, although the borrower may choose to have a prepayment clause included in the financing contract.

Washington

Office of Small Business
Washington Department of Trade and Economic Development
General Administration Building
Olympia, WA 98504
Phone: (206) 753-5614
Description: Furnishes information to small businesses through seminars, publications, and general counseling. Assists firms wishing to provide goods and services to state agencies. Clients who are in need of more in-depth management and technical assistance will be referred to appropriate organizations for help.

Small Business Development Centers
Small Business Development Center
College of Business and Economics
Washington State University
Pullman, WA 99164
Phone: (509) 335-1576
Description: Provides assistance with new business formation through manufacturing counseling, market research, financial

STARTING A NEW BUSINESS IN ARKANSAS

A publication of the

ARKANSAS SMALL BUSINESS DEVELOPMENT CENTER

Virginia Business Opportunities

Tells you what products and services the Commonwealth of Virginia is buying and selling.

Don't miss an opportunity to bid.

What You Need To Know About

Tax Deferrals and Credits

for
Distressed Areas •
New Businesses •

Washington State
Department of Revenue
William R. Wilkerson
Director

counseling, new products evaluation and testing, feasibility studies, and organizational analyses.

West Virginia

West Virginia Division of Small Business
Small Business Division
State Capitol Complex
Charleston, WV 25305
Phone: (304) 348-2960 (In West Virginia, call 1-800-CALL-WVA)
Description: Assists small businesses with the filing of state and federal forms by providing a one-stop resource center. Their programs include managerial and technical assistance, financial resources and loan packaging, education and training, procurement, advocacy, legislation, and Minority Business Enterprise/Women-owned Business Enterprise Program.

West Virginia Development Authority Direct Loans
Small Business Division
State Capitol Complex
Charleston, WV 25305
Phone: (304) 348-2960 (In West Virginia, call 1-800-CALL-WVA)
Description: Funding provided for up to 50% of projects at low interest rates with flexible terms. Maximum loan amount is $500,000.

West Virginia Certified Development Corporation
Small Business Division
State Capitol Complex
Charleston, WV 25303
Phone: (304) 384-2960 (In West Virginia, call 1-800-CALL-WVA)
Description: Small and medium sized businesses are provided with long-term, fixed-rate loans. Interest rates will be tied to rates on U.S. Treasury Bills at the time the loan is made. Maximum loan amount is $500,000.

Wisconsin

Small Business Development Centers

Small Business Development Center
602 State Street
Madison, WI 53703-1099
Phone: (608) 263-7766
Description: Provides free information and assistance for small businesspeople wishing to start or expand their business. Individual counseling is available.

Customized Labor-Training Funds

Wisconsin Department of Development
123 West Washington Avenue
Madison, WI 53702
Phone: (608) 266-1018
Description: Provides training for Wisconsin workers to provide the skilled labor required for business development and employment.

Permit Information Center

Wisconsin Department of Development, Permit Information Center
123 West Washington Avenue
PO Box 7970
Madison, WI 53707
Phone: (608) 266-1018 (In Wisconsin, call 1-800-HELP-BUS)
Description: Provides information on obtaining all permits necessary to do business in Wisconsin.

Wisconsin Department of Development

Wisconsin Department of Development
123 West Washington Avenue
PO Box 7970
Madison, WI 53707
Phone: (608) 266-1018
Description: Provides a complete listing and brief description of the numerous federal, state, and local financing programs available to businesses. Financing may be used for long-term capital, working capital, unforeseen damages, export financing, research grants, and labor training.

Small Enterprise Economic Development (Seed) Program

Wisconsin Housing and Economic Development Authority
James Wilson Plaza, Suite 300
131 West Wilson Street
Madison, WI 53701-1728
Phone: (608) 266-7884

Description: Offers long-term, fixed rate financing to small and medium sized businesses at rates lower than the prime. Eligible borrowers must be businesses or individuals associated with a business which has a current gross annual sales figure of $35 million or less, a satisfactory credit history, and an ability to support debt service. SEED money can be used for the purchase, expansion, and improvement of land, plant, and equipment as well as for depreciable research and development expenditures, so long as such projects result in the creation and maintenance of jobs.

Wisconsin Business Development Finance Corporation

Wisconsin Business Development Finance Corporation
PO Box 2717
Madison, WI 53701-2717
Phone: (608) 258-8830

Description: Participates with financial institutions to provide small business with financing for up to 25 years. Funds can be used to purchase land and buildings and machinery and equipment and for construction and modernization of facilities. Financing can vary from $100,000 to $500,000. Interest rates are less than conventional financing.

Wyoming

Small Business Institute

Institute of Business and Management Services
College of Commerce and Industry
PO Box 3275
University Station, University of Wyoming
Laramie, WY 82071
Phone: (307) 766-2363

Description: The institute works to match small businesses with upper level business students and faculty in the University of Wyoming's College of Commerce and Industry. A typical

112

management team consists of two students and one faculty member, with expertise in the project's area. They work as a team in whatever type of business consultation is required by the business. This service is provided at no charge by the Wyoming business community.

Wyoming Business Development Center

944 East Second Street
Casper, WY 82601
Phone: (307) 766-2363
Description: Provides free counseling service, seminars, and management classes to small businesses.

Job Training Partnership Act

Division of Manpower Planning
Barrett Building
Cheyenne, WY 82002
Phone: (307) 777-7671
Description: Funds are provided to support worker training and retraining. Can provide direct subsidies for as much as 50% of wages during training and support services.

Wyoming Department of Economic Planning and Development

Wyoming Department of Economic Planning and Development
Herschler Building
Cheyenne, WY 82002
Phone: (307) 777-7285 (In Wyoming, call 1-800-262-3425)
Description: Offers a wide variety of funding programs, including: Block Grants, Industrial Revenue Bonds, Small Business Administration 503 Loan Program, and many others.

Capital Corporation of Wyoming, INC.

Capital Corporation of Wyoming, INC.
PO Box 612
Casper, WY 82602
Phone: (307) 234-5438
Description: Financing for facility construction and expansion, shops and warehouses, office and equipment inventory, and venture capital. Also provides equity financing to new and expanding business.

Local Development Companies
Wyoming Department of Economic Planing and Development
Herschler Building
Cheyenne, WY 82002
Phone: (307) 777-7285 (Call toll-free, 1-800-262-3425)
Description: Provides financial assistance as well as information on sites, buildings, and other capital goods available for firms in their area. They work with private funds raised by sale of stock, contributions, subscriptions, or by notes of indebtedness. There are approximately 28 local development companies in Wyoming.

Chapter Three

Special SBA Programs

Many of the state programs listed earlier, especially the ones providing loans and loan-guarantees, are funded by a department of the federal government, The Small Business Association. The various state agencies administer these federal funds on a local level. What follows is list of all the ways the SBA can help you and your new business. Most are administered through one or more of the various agencies operating in your state. When you see a program you are interested in, contact an agency in your state and inquire about how it works. If that particular program isn't available in your state, or not available through a state agency, contact the nearest SBA office directly. The regional offices of the SBA are listed later in this chapter.

SBI

The Small Business Institute program is a small business counseling program offered at 530 colleges and universities. Through this program, small businesses are provided in-depth management counseling by teams of senior and graduate level business students under the guidance of a faculty advisory. Check with the programs in your state (listed earlier) for more information.

CDC

The Certified Development Corporation, known as CDC, is a private, nonprofit organization which arranges low-interest loans for small and medium-sized businesses in an effort to strengthen the local economy. The CDC is chartered by the SBA and also is supported by various government agencies. Information about these programs also can be found by calling your state programs.

CDC is one of more than 500 such development corporations in the U.S. sanctioned by the SBA. Since its certification in 1980, CDC has consistently been ranked by the SBA as the leader in:

- *Loans processed.*
- *Dollar amount of loans funded.*
- *Number of jobs created and preserved.*

What kinds of loans does CDC offer?

- *Expansion*
- *Remodeling*
- *Acquisition of the building you're now leasing*
- *Purchase of a building or construction site.*
- *Working capital.*
- *Inventory.*
- *Debt consolidation.*
- *Fixtures and equipment*
- *Business start ups.*
- *Updating your equipment*

In fact, funds are available for almost any valid business purpose.

How much can I borrow?:

CDC can arrange loans up to $5.5 million

To Apply:

Contact the CDC office and talk with a representative. The staff at the state offices will be able to fill you in about how much and what kind of loans are available. CDC's loan developers help companies to determine what type of financial support is best, and then help the loan applicant secure the participation of a financial institution and negotiate with any third parties to expedite the loan process.

Approximately 98 percent of qualified applications are approved for funding.

Here are the specific SBA programs from which much of the state help mentioned earlier is funded.

The 504 Loan Program:

The 504 Debenture Loan Program allows the business owner to purchase, construct or remodel an industrial or commercial building. Financing is at below-market interest rates with only 10 percent down payment or equity injection. The loans are a mixture of private capital and federal debenture funds. Private financial institutions participate for as little as 50 percent of the total project cost. CDC finances 40 percent or $500,000 - whichever is less. Total project costs may include related "soft costs."

The CDC Debenture is guaranteed 100 percent by the SBA. It is for terms of 10 or 20 years at a fixed interest rate determined on the date of the sale of the debenture.

Eligibility for the 504 Program is limited to "for profit" corporations, partnerships or proprietorships with a minimum business history of one year, a net worth not to exceed $6 million, or net profit in excess of $2 million after taxes for two consecutive years. CDC also can recommend alternative financing programs which may better meet a company's needs.

Benefits of 504 Loan Financing include:

- *Low down payment*
- *Reduced interest rates*
- *Longer terms*
- *Preservation of working capital*
- *Easy to qualify*
- *Tax advantages to principals*

118

Some facts to keep in mind:

1) A guarantee of repayment must be provided.

2) For every $15,000 of CDC funds, one job must be preserved or created.

3) Your company must occupy at least 51% of the building space within an existing building.

4) Your company must occupy 85% of the building space in new construction.

5) CDC funds may only be applied to that portion of the building occupied by your company.

6) A CDC legal fee is charged in all 504 loans.

7) A prepayment penalty may be charged.

8) CDC's loan is based on bank's appraisal.

9) Loan assumptions are at the discretion of the lender(s).

The 7a Loan Program:

CDC arranges loans up to $550,000 or 90 percent of a loan for small businesses through the SBA. One-to-six-year loans are at a maximum rate of 2 1/4 percent above the prime rate. Loans from 7 to 25 years mature at the maximum rate of 2 3/4 percent above the prime rate. The loan is usually limited to 7 years for working capital financing, 10 years for purchasing equipment, and 25 years for construction or for purchasing land and buildings. The SBA and the lender require a new business applicant to put up a "reasonable amount" of the project's cost, depending on the loan request and the borrower's ability to repay the loan. Fixed assets, real estate, and inventory are taken as security.

Loans can be obtained for:

- *Business start-ups*
- *Business acquisition*

- *Real estate*
- *Equipment purchases*
- *Working Capital*
- *Debt consolidation*
- *Inventory*
- *Leasehold Improvements*
- *Other business purposes*

Collateral:
Security for 7a loans can be one or more of the following:

- *A mortgage on equipment and/or fixtures.*
- *Assignment of receivables and inventory.*
- *Personal guarantees of officers, directors, and stockholders.*
- *A mortgage on personal and/or business real estate.*

Handicapped Assistance Loans

This program arranges low interest loans and guarantees to public or private nonprofit organizations operating in the interest of handicapped individuals. Businesses owned by handicapped individuals may also qualify for financing through this program. Guaranteed loans are limited to $350,000 with a maximum term of 25 years. Direct loans are made for up to $100,000.

The Energy Loan Program

Assists small businesses that develop, manufacture, sell, install, or service specific solar energy and energy-saving devices. Applicants must indicate projected and actual energy savings and the number of jobs created by the business. Direct loans are made for up to $150,000, and loan guarantees for up to $500,000. Terms may be extended for up to 25 years.

Disaster Recovery Loans

Assist businesses that have suffered either physical damage or economic injury from a natural disaster. To qualify, a business must be located in a region officially declared a disaster by the President, Secretary of Agriculture, or Administrator of the SBA. Physical disaster loans (other than home loans) may not exceed a maximum of $500,000. This type of loan generally carries lower than market interest rates. Disaster loans may be extended for up to 30 years, and repayment usually begins 5 months from the date of the loan.

Seasonal Lines of Credit

Guarantee loans to finance a seasonal increase in business activity. Amounts are similar to those under 7a. Although a business may have other SBA loans outstanding, only one seasonal loan can be outstanding at any one time. Seasonal lines of credit are not revolving; each loan must be repaid within 12 months and be followed by an out-of-debt period of at least 30 days. Seasonal loans, secured by inventory and accounts receivable, are paid when assets are liquidated. Credit can be used only for labor and materials, and the client must show sufficient working capital to cover expenses. Prior to the termination date, the bank and/or the SBA will review the contract, at which time the line of credit may be reduced or extended.

Export Revolving Lines of Credit

Guarantee lines of credit extended by lenders to small businesses engaged in exporting. Amounts are similar to those in the 7a loan guarantee program. Funds may be used for labor and materials and to penetrate or develop foreign markets; they may not be used to pay existing obligations or to purchase fixed assets. Borrowers must have been in business (not necessarily in exporting) for at least 12 months prior to filing an application. The term of the loan is based on the borrower's delivery requirements but may not exceed 18 months.

SBA Criteria Or Collateral

Because the SBA serves businesses not bankable without its guarantee, clients are obviously intermediate risks. They may be undercapitalized, lack sufficient collateral, and have a minimal track record or imperfect operating history. Or, they may require a repayment period that is longer than lenders may be willing to extend in order to accommodate projected cash flow. To curb its lending risks, the SBA sets modest loan ceilings and offers clients free management assistance. Interest rates on its guaranteed loans cannot exceed maximums set by the SBA. The interest on hard-to-get direct loans is normally slightly below comparable bank rates.

The SBA's loan documentation requirements are generally more complex than that of a bank. Applications for SBA loan guarantees are first reviewed by the lender and, if approved, passed to the SBA. Like banks, the SBA must first be convinced that a business can repay the loan from profits. Consequently, the SBA is interested in profitability ratios and business projections. But unlike commercial lenders, the SBA will sometimes ignore a losing track record if the business shows signs of improvement leading to a healthy future. The SBA also will make loans for longer maturities than bank loans and accept borrowers whose collateral does not support the full value of the loan.

Processing for term loan guarantees normally takes two to three weeks after receiving approval from the lender. Since seasonal line-of-credit applicants are typically established customers, the SBA often can process these guarantees in less time. Direct loans may require several weeks' processing time.

Certified Lenders

In an effort to reduce paperwork and streamline the delivery of financial services to small businesses, the SBA initiated the Certified Lenders Program (CLP) in 1979. Under the CLP, the lender performs an initial credit analysis of applications and then forwards them to the SBA for final approval. Under the newer Preferred Lenders Program (PLP), credit authority is delegated to the lender. Preferred lenders make final approvals on loan requests and then report them to the SBA, which guarantees up to 75 percent of the borrowed amount. PLP loans are guaranteed for a minimum of $100,000 and a maximum of $500,000. Interest rates are negotiable between borrower and lender. Preferred landers can normally process loan requests in a matter of days.

Small Business Administration Regional Offices

Alabama

2121 8th Ave. North
Suite 200
Birmingham, AL 35203-2398
(205) 731-1344

Alaska

Room 1068, Module G
8th & C Street
Anchorage, AK 99501
(907)271-4022

Arizona

2005 North Central Avenue
5th Floor
Phoenix, AZ 85004
(602) 241-3732

300 West Congress Street
Box FB - 33
Tuscon, AZ 85701
(602) 629-6715

Arkansas

320 W. Capitol Avenue
Suite 601
Little Rock, AR 72201
(501) 378-5871

California

450 Golden Gate Avenue
Box 36044
San Francisco, CA 94102
(415) 974-0599

350 S. Figueroa Street
Sixth Floor
Los Angeles, CA 90071
(213) 894-2956

2202 Monterey Street
Suite 108
Fresno, CA 93721
(209) 487-5189

880 Front Street
Suite 4-S-29
San Diego, CA 92188
(619) 557-7250

660 J Street, Suite 215
Sacramento, CA 95814
(916) 551-1446

Fidelity Federal Building
2700 North Main Street
Suite 400
Santa Ana, CA 92701
(617) 472-2494

Colorado

Executive Tower Building
1405 Curtis Street
22nd Floor
Denver, CO 80202-2395
(303) 844-5441

721 - 19th Street
Room 420
Denver, CO 80202-2599
(303) 844-2607

Connecticut

330 Main Street
2nd Floor
Hartford, CT 06106
(203) 722-3600

Delaware

844 King Street, Room 5207
Lockbox 16
Wilmington, DE 19801
(302) 573-6294

District Of Columbia

1111 - 18th Street, N.W.
Sixth Floor
P.O. Box 19993
Washington, DC 20036
(202)634-4950

Florida

400 West Bay Street
Box 35067
Jacksonville, FL 32202
(904) 791-3782

1320 S. Dixie HIghway
Suite 501
Coral Gables, FL 33136
(305) 536-5521

700 Twigs Street
Room 607
Tampa, FL 33136
(305) 689-2223

Georgia

1375 Peachtree Street, N.E.
5th Floor
Atlanta, GA 30367-8102
(404) 347-2441

1720 Peachtree Road, N.W.
6th Floor
Atlanta, GA 30309
(404) 347-2441

Federal Bldg., Room 225
52 North Main Street
Statesboro, GA 30458
(912) 489-8719

Guam

Pacific News Bldg., Rm. 508
238 O'Hara Street
Agana, Guam 96910
(671) 472-7277

Hawaii

300 Ala Moana
Room 2213
P.O. Box 50207
Honolulu, HI 96850
(808) 541-2977

Idaho

1020 Main Street
Suite 290
Boise, ID 83702
(208) 334-1696

Illinois

230 South Dearborn St.
Room 510
Chicago, IL 60604
(312) 353-4252

219 South Dearborn St.
Room 437
Chicago, IL 60605
(312) 353-4528

Washington Building
Four North Old State
Capitol Plaza
Springfield, IL 62701
(217) 492-4416

Indiana

575 N. Pennsylvania Street
Room 578
Indianapolis, IN 46204-1584
(317) 269-7272

Iowa

210 Walnut Street, COM
Des Moines, IA 50309
(515) 284-4760

373 Collins Road, N.E.
Cedar Rapids, IA 52402
(319) 269-6191

Kentucky

Federal Office Bldg.
600 Federal Place
Room 188
Louisville, KY 40202
(502) 582-5976

Louisiana

Ford-Fisk Bldg.
1661 Canal Street
2nd Floor
New Orleans, LA 70112
(504) 589-6685

Federal Bldg. & Courthouse
500 Fannin Street
Room 6B14
Shreveport, LA 71101
(318) 226-5196

Maine

40 Western Avenue
Federal Bldg. Room 512
Augusta, ME 04330
(207) 622-8378

Maryland

10 N. Calvert St.
3rd Floor
Baltimore MD 21202
(301) 962-4392

Massachusetts

60 Batterymarch Street
10th Floor
Boston, MA 02110
(617) 223-3204

10 Causeway Street
Room 265
Boston, MA 02114
(617) 565-5590

Federal Bldg. & Courthouse
1550 Main St. Room 212
Springfield, MA 01103
(413) 785-0268

Michigan

McNamara Bldg.
477 Michigan Avenue
Room 515
Detroit, MI 48226
(313) 226-6075

220 W. Washington St.
Marguette, MI 49885
(906) 225-1108

Minnesota

610-C Butler Square
100 North 6th Street

Minneapolis, MN 55403
(612) 349-3574

Mississippi

Dr. A.H. McCoy Federal Bldg.
100 West Capitol Street
Suite 322
Jackson, MS 39269
(601) 965-4378

One Hancock Plaza
Suite 1001
Gulfport, MS 39501-7758
(601) 863-4449

Missouri

911 Walnut Street
13th Floor
Kansas City, MO 64106
(816) 374-5311
1103 Grand Avenue
6th Floor
Kansas City, MO 64106
(816) 374-5868

815 Olive Street
Room 242
St. Louis, MO 63101
(314) 425-6600

339 Broadway
Room 140
Cape Girardeau, Mo 63701
(314) 335-6039

The Landmark Building
309 North Jefferson
Springfield, MO 65805
(417) 864-7670

Montana

301 South Park Avenue
Room 528
Drawer 10054
Helena, MT 59626
(406) 449-5381

Post Ofc. Bldg. Rm. 216
2601 First Avenue North
Billings, MT 59101
(406) 657-6047

Nebraska

11145 Mill Valley Road
Omaha, NE 68154
(402) 221-4691

Nevada

Box 7527-Downtown Sta.
301 East Stewart
Las Vegas, NV 89125
(702) 388-6019

50 S. Virginia Street
Room 238
P.O. Box 3216
Reno, NV 889505
(702) 784-5268

New Hampshire

55 Pleasant Street
Room 209
P.O. Box 1257
Concord, NH 03301
(603) 225-1400

New Jersey

60 Park Place
4th Floor
Newark, NJ 07102
(201) 645-2434

2600 Mt. Ephrain Avenue
Camden, NJ 08104
(609) 757-5184

New Mexico

Patio Plaza Bldg., Suite 320
5000 Marble Ave., N.E.
Albuquerque, NM 87110

New York
26 Federal Plaza
Room 29-118
New York, NY 10278
(212) 264-7772

26 Federal Plaza
Room 3100
New York, NY 10278
(212) 264-4355

445 Broadway
Room 236-B
Albany, NY 12207
(518) 472-6300

111 West Huron Street
Room 1311
Buffalo, NY 14202
(716) 846-4301

333 East Water St.
Room 412

Elmira, NY 14901
(607) 734-8130

35 Pinelawn Road
Room 102-E
Melville, NY 11747
(516) 454-0750

Federal Bldg. - Room 601
100 State Street
Rochester, NY 14614
(716) 263-6700

Federal Bldg. - Room 1071
100 South Clinton St.
Syracuse, NY 13260
(315) 423-5383

North Carolina

222 South Church Street
Roon 300
Charlotte, NC 28202
(704) 371-6563

North Dakota

Federal Bldg. Room 218
657 Second Avenue, North
P.O. Box 3086
Fargo, ND 58102
(701) 237-5131

Ohio
AJC Federal Bldg. Room 317
1240 East 9th Street
Cleveland, OH 44199
(216) 522-4180

Federal Bldg. U.S. Courthouse

85 Marconi Blvd. Rm. 512
Columbus, OH 43215
(614) 469-6860

John Weld Peck Fed. Bldg.
550 Main Street
Room 5028
Cincinnati, OH 45202
(513) 684-2814

Oklahoma

200 N.W. 5th Street
Suite 670
Oklahoma City, OK 73102
(405) 231-4494

Oregon

Federal Bldg., Roon 676
1220 S.W. Third Ave.
Portland, OR 97204-2882
(503) 423-5221

Pennsylvania

One Bala Cynwyd Plaza
231 St. Asaphs Road
Suite 640 West
Bala Cynwyd, PA 19004
(512) 596-5889

One Bala Cynwyd Road
231 St. Asaphs Road
Suite 400 East
Bala Cynwyd, PA 19004
(215) 596-5822

100 Chestnut Street
Roon 309

Harrisburg, PA 17101
(717) 782-3840

960 Penn Avenue
5th Floor
Pittsburgh, PA 15222
(412) 644-2780

Penn Place
20 N. Pennsylvania Ave.
Room 2327
Wilkes-Barre, PA 18701
(717) 826-6497

Puerto Rico

Federico Degatau Fed. Bldg.
Room 691
Carlos Chardon Avenue
Hato Rey, PR 00918
(809) 753-4002

Rhode Island
380 Westminster Mall
Providence, RI 02903
(401) 528-4586

South Carolina

1835 Assembly Street
3rd Floor
P.O. Box 2786
Columbia, SC 29202
(803) 765-5376

South Dakota

101 South Main Avenue
Suite 101, Security Bldg.

Sioux Falls, SD 57102-0577
(605) 336-2980, Ext. 231

Tennessee

404 James Robertson Pkwy.
Suite 1012, Parkway Towers
Nashville, TN 37219
(615) 736-5881

Texas

8625 King George Drive
Bldg. C
Dallas TX 75235-3391
(214) 767-0495

Federal Building
Room 780
300 East 8th Street
Austin, TX 78701
(512) 482-5288

819 Taylor Street
Room 10A27
Ft. Worth, TX 76102
(817) 334-3613

400 Mann Street
Suite 403
Corpus Christi, TX 78401
(512) 888-3331

10737 Gateway West
Suite 320
El Paso, TX 79935
(915) 541-7560

222 E. Van Buren St.
Suite 500
Harlingen, TX 78550

(512) 423-8934

2525 Murworth
Suite 112
Houston, TX 77054
(713) 660-4420

1611 10th Street
Suite 200
Lubbock, TX 79401
(806) 743-7481

100 South Washington St.
Room G-12, Federal Bldg.
Marshall, TX 75670
(214) 935-5257

Federal Bldg., Room A-513
727 E. Durango Street
San Antonio, TX 78206
(512) 229-6272

Utah

125 South State Street
Room 2237
Salt Lake City, UT 84138-1195
(801) 524-3209

Vermont

87 State Street
Room 205
Montpelier, VT 05602
(802) 828-4474

Virginia

400 North 8th Street
Room 3015

P.O. Box 10126
Richmond, VA 23240
(804) 771-2765

Virgin Islands

Veterans Drive
Room 210, Federal Bldg.
St. Thomos, VI 00801
(809) 774-8530

4C & 4D Estate Sion Farm
Room 7
P.O. Box 4010
Christiansted
St. Croix, VI 00820
(809) 773-3480

Washington

Fourth & Vine Bldg.
2615 Fourth Avenue
Room 440
Seattle, WA 98121
(206) 442-1456

915 Second Avenue
Room 1792
Seattle, WA 98174
(206) 442-5534

U.S. Courthouse, Room 651
P.O. Box 2167
Spokane, WA 99210
(509) 456-3786

West Virginia

168 West Main Street
5th Floor
Clarksburg, WV 26301
(304) 623-5631

550 Eagan Street
Room 309
Charleston, WV 25301
(304) 347-5220

Wisconsin

212 E. Washington Ave.
Room 213
Madison, WI 53703
(608) 264-5205

Henry S. Reuss Federal Plaza
310 W. Wisconsin Avenue
Suite 400
Milwaukee, WI 53203
(414) 291-3942

Federal Ofc. Bldg. & U.S. Courthouse
500 South Barstow Street
Room 17
Eau Claire, WI 54701
(715) 834-9012

Wyoming

100 East B Street
Federal Bldg., Room 40001
P.O. Box 2839
Casper, WY 82602-2839
(307) 261-5761

SBICs

Small Business Investment Companies(SBIC) are privately managed firms that are licensed and partially financed by the SBA. The SBIC program is the only venture capital program sponsored by the Federal Government. SBICs were created to provide equity capital and long term loans to small firms. They can furnish your business with the money it needs in one of two ways: either by a straight loan, or a stock investment in your company (or a combination of the two). Each SBIC has its own rules and regulations but all transactions are regulated by the government. SBICs primarily assist small firms with significant growth potential or new small firms in innovative industries.

One specialized type of SBIC licensee is called 301(d) (known as Minority Enterprise SBICs). The 301(d) SBICs provide help solely to small firms owned by socially and economically disadvantaged persons. Since the SBIC program started in 1958, some 85,000 financings have been made for over $6.3 billion.

SBICs invest in all types of manufacturing and service industries. Many investment companies seek out small businesses with new products or services, because of the strong growth potential of such firms. Some SBICs specialize in the field in which their management has special knowledge or competency. Most, however, consider a wide variety of investment opportunities.

Only firms defined by the SBA as "small" are eligible for SBIC financing. The SBA defines small businesses as companies whose net worth is $6.0 million or less, and whose average net (after tax) income for the preceding two years does not exceed $2.0 million. For business in industries for which these standards are too low, alternative size standards are available.

Keep in mind that SBICs are businesses and that they are looking for profits just like you. Their success depends upon the growth and profits of the companies in which they own stock (remember SBICs often receive stock from companies in exchange for monies lent). To protect their investment, they frequently offer management advice and services as well.

Many small businesses are eligible for SBIC loans, and if a business is at least 50 percent minority owned, the chances for a loan are even better.

Similar to SBA loans (funds directly from the government), SBIC loans usually carry lower interest rates than those offered by commercial banks, and repayment is spread out over a longer time period.

There are thousands of SBIC companies around the country. We have listed as many as we could find, but there are new ones forming all the time. Check your local library for books which catalog information on SBIC companies, like their requirements and the areas in which they deal. **Also, your local SBA office will provide you with a SBIC directory that contains all the companies in your area.**

Unless you live in the boon docks, you probably will have more than one SBIC to choose from. In this case, it is necessary to evaluate the ones in your proximity and pick the one that best suits your business. Many SBICs invest in a wide variety of industries, but others are selective and specialize in specific markets. Being the persistent, dedicated entrepreneur you are, you must leave no stone unturned in presenting your proposal to every possible SBIC in your area. However, if your research tells you that company "X" invests **only** in porcelain bathtub manufacturers, and this is not your field, then it's safe to say you're wasting your time with them.

In choosing an SBIC, consult local attorneys, bankers, accountants, business associates and advisors who may have had contact with SBICs before. Learn as much as you can about the different SBICs in your area, because each firm differs. Four qualities to look for are:

1. How much do they have available for investment?

2. Do they offer management services?

3. What types of investments to they make?

4. Can they offer additional financing later?

141

Additional assistance and counseling is available for women business owners, minorities, and disabled citizens. While you should definitely take advantage of the services that are provided to you, don't use them as your only source. This chapter is filled with other alternatives for money and advice and the most successful people are those who investigate every option.

When you've identified the SBICs you think are best suited for financing for your company, you'll need to prepare for a presentation. Your initial presentation will play a major role in successfully to obtaining financing. Briefly, it's up to you to demonstrate that an investment in your firm is worthwhile. The best way to achieve this is to present a detailed and comprehensive business plan.

MESBICs

In 1969, the U.S. Small Business Administration, in cooperation with the U.S. Department of Commerce, created **Minority Enterprise Small Business Investment Companies** (MESBICs or 301(d) licensees) to serve only those small businesses that were at least 51 percent owned by socially or economically disadvantaged Americans.

Like SBICs, MESBICs are licensed and regulated by the federal government under the SBA. They must be privately capitalized with at least $1 million in assets. Then they are eligible for $3 to $4 of SBA funding for every dollar of private capital. Most SBICs and MESBICs are owned by small groups of individuals. A few are publicly owned, and corporations and financial institutions own the rest.

SBIC and MESBIC investments are ordinarily smaller than those of their larger, privately funded counterparts. By federal regulations, MESBICs may spend up to 30 percent of their private capital on a single investment. In contrast, SBICs may spend only 20 percent of their private capital on a single client.

These investment companies normally purchase common and preferred stock or limited partnership interests in their clients' small businesses. However, because companies must pay interest

142

on funds received from the SBA, they often opt for incom-
egenerating debentures or loans with warrants over straight equity investments.

The majority of these investment companies prefer to finance expanding businesses rather than those just starting out, and they
look for an annually compounded return of at least 20 percent on
an investment. Generally, SBICs and MESBICs expect to divest
themselves of their interest in a business within five to seven
years.

SBICs and MESBICs scrutinize the business plan like any other
venture capitalist. Basically they are looking for growth potential
in a healthy industry, sound management, and a proven track
record.

Minority Business Development Agencies

Regional and District Offices

Los Angeles, CA 90012
977 Broadway, Suite 201
(213) 894-7157

New York, NY 10278
26 Federal Plaza, Suite 37-20
(212) 264-3262

San Francisco, CA 94105
221 Main St. 12th Floor
(415) 974-9597

Atlanta, GA 30309
1371 Peachtree St. NE, Suite 505
(404) 347-4091

Philadelphia, PN 19108
W.J. Green Federal Bldg. Room 9436
(215) 597-9236

Dallas, TX 75242
1100 Commerce St. Suite 7B-19

(214) 767-8001

Washington D.C. 20230
14th and Pennsylvania Ave. Suite 5714
(202) 377-1958

Directory of Small Business Investment Companies

This directory is an alphabetical listing by state of Small Business Investment Companies (including branch offices). The listed companies have recieved licenses from the SBA and their licenses remain outstanding. This list does not include currently licensed SBICs that are in the process of surrendering their licenses or that are subject to legal proceedings that might terminate their licenses.

Alabama
First SBIC of Alabama
David Delaney, President
16 Midtown Park East
Mobile, AL 36606
(205) 476-0700 Diversified

Hickory Venture Capital Corporation
J. Thomas Noojin, President
699 Gallatin Street, Suite A-2
Huntsville, AL 35801
(205) 539-1931 Diversified

Remington Fund, Inc.
Lana Sellers, President
1927 First Avenue North
Birmingham, AL 35202
(205) 324-7709 Diversified

Alaska
Alaska Business Investment Corp.
James Cloud, Vice President
301 West Northern Lights Blvd.

Mail: P.O. Box 100600; Anchorage 99510
Anchorage, AK 99510
(907) 278-2071 Diversified

Arizona

Norwest Venture Partners
(Main Office: Minneapolis, MN)
88777 E. Via de Ventura
Suite 335
Scottsdale, AZ 85258
(602) 483-8940

Northwest Growth Fund, Inc.
(Main Office: Minneapolis, MN)
88777 E. Via de Ventura
Suite 335
Scottsdale, AZ 85258
(602) 483-8940

Rocky Mountain Equity Corporation
Anthony J. Nicoli, President
4530 Central Avenue
Phoenix, AZ 85012
(602) 274-7534 Diversified

Valley National Investors, Inc.
Harley Barnes, President
201 North Central Avenue, Suite 900
Phoenix, AZ 85004
(602) 261-1577 Diversified

Wilbur Venture Capital Corp.
Jerry F. Wilbur, President
4575 South Palo Verde, Suite 305
Tucson, AZ 85714
(602) 747-5999 Diversified

Arkansas

Independence Financial Services, Inc.
Jeffrey Hance, General Manager
Town Plaza Office Park

Mail: P.O. Box 3878
Batesville, AR 72501
(501) 793-4533 Diversified

Small Business Investment Capital, Inc.
Charles E. Toland, President
10003 New Benton Hwy.
Mail: P.O. Box 3627
Little Rock, AR 72203
(501) 455-3590 Grocery Stores

California

AMF Financial Inc.
William Temple, Vice President
4330 La Jolla Village Drive
Suite 110
San Diego, CA 92122
(619) 546-0167 Diversified

Atalanta Investment Company, Inc.
(Main Office: New York, NY)
141 El Camino Drive
Beverly Hills, CA 90212
(213) 273-1730

BNP Venture Capital Corporation
Edgerton Scott II, President
3000 Sand Hill Road
Building 1, Suite 125
Menlo Park, CA 94025
(415) 854-1084 Diversified

Bancorp Venture Capital, Inc.
Arthur H. Bernstein, President
11812 San Vicente Boulevard
Los Angeles, CA 90049
(213) 820-7222 Diversified

BankAmerica Ventures, Inc.
Patrick Topolski, President
555 California Street
San Francisco, CA 94104
(4150 953-3001

CFB Venture Capital Corporation
(Main Office: San Diego, CA)
350 California Street, Mexxanine
San Francisco, CA 94104
(415) 445-0594

California Capital Investors, Ltd.
Arthur H. Bernstein, Managing G.P.
11812 San Vincente Blvd.

Los Angeles, CA 90049
(213) 820-7222 Diversified

Citicorp Venture Capital, Ltd.
(Main Office: New York, NY)
2 Embarcadero Place
2200 Geny Road, Suite 203
Palo Alto, Ca 94303
(415) 424-8000

City Ventures, Inc.
Warner Heineman, Vice Chairman
400 N. Roxbury Drive
Beverly Hills, CA 90210
(213) 550-5709 Diversified

Crosspoint Investment Corporation
Max Simpson, Pres. & Chief F.O.
1951 Landings Drive
Mountain View, CA 94043
(415) 968-0930 Diversified

Developers Equity Capital Corporation
Larry Sade, Chairman of the Board
1880 Century Park East
Suite 311
Los Angeles, CA 90067
(213) 277-0330 100 percent Real Estate

Draper Associates, a California LP
Bill Edwards, President
c/o Timothy C. Draper
3000 Sand Hill Road, Bldg. 4, #235
Menlo Park, CA 94025
(415) 854-1712 Diversified

First Interstate Capital, Inc.
Ronald J. Hall, Managing Director
5000 Birch Street, Suite 10100
Newport Beach, CA 92660
(714) 253-4360 Diversified

First SBIC of California
Tim Hay, President
650 Town Center Drive
Seventeenth Floor
Costa Mesa, CA 92626
(714) 556-1964 Diversified

First SBIC of California
(Main Office: Costa Mesa, CA)
155 North Lake Avenue, Suite 1010
Pasadena, CA 91109
(818) 304-3451

First SBIC of California
(Main Office: Costa Mesa, CA)
5 Palo Alto Square, Suite 938
Palo Alto, CA 94306
(415)424-8011

G C & H Partners
James C. Gaither, General Partner
One Maritime Plaza, 20th Floor
San Francisco, CA 94110
(415) 981-5252 Diversified

HMS Capital, Ltd.
Michael Hone, President
555 California Street, Room 5070
San Francisco, CA 94109
(415) 221-1225 Diversified

Hamco Capital Corp.
William R. Hambrecht, President
235 Montgomery Street
San Francisco, CA 94104
(415) 986-6567 Diversified

Imperial Ventures, Inc.
H. Wayne Snavely, President
9920 South La Cienega Blvd.
Mail: P.O. Box 92991; L.A. 90009
Inglewood, CA 90301
(213)417-5888 Diversified

Ivanhoe Venture Capital, Ltd.
Alan Toffler, General Partner
737 Pearl Street, Suite 201
La Jolla, CA 92037
(619) 454-8882

Jupiter Partners
John M. Bryan, President
600 Montgomery Street
35th Floor
San Francisco, CA 94111
(415) 421-9990

Marwit Capital COrp.
Martin W. Witte, President
180 Newport Center Drive
Suite 200
Newport Beach, CA 92660
(714) 640-6234 Diversified

Merrill Pickard Anderson & Eyre
Steven L. Merrill, President
Two Palo Alto Square, Suite 425
Palo Alto, CA 94306
(415) 856-8880 Diversified

Metropolitan Venture Company, Inc.
Rudolph J. Lowy, Chairman of the Board
5757 Wilshire Blvd.
Suite 670
Los Angeles, CA 90036
(213) 938-3488 Diversified

Nelson Capital Corp.
(Main OFfice: Garden City, NY)
10000 Santa Monica Blvd., Suite 300
Los Angeles, CA 90067
(213)556-1944

New West Partners
Timothy P. Haidinger, Manager
4350 Executive Drive, Suite 206

San Diego, CA 92121
(619) 457-0723 Diversified

New West Partners
(Main Office: San Diego, CA)
4600 Campus Drive, Suite 103
Newport Beach, CA 92660
(714) 756-8940

PBC Venture Capital Inc.
Henry L. Wheeler, Manager
1408 - 18th Street
Mail: P.O. Box 6008; Bakersfield 93386
Bakersfield, CA 93301
(805) 395-3555 Diversified

Peerless Capital Company, Inc.
Robert W. Lautz, Jr., President
675 South Arroyo Parkway
Suite 320
Pasadena, CA 91105
(818) 577-9199 Diversified

Ritter Partners
William C. Edwards, President
150 Isabella Avenue
Atherton, CA 94025
(415) 392-7500

Round Table Capital Corporation
Richard Dumke, President
655 Montgomery Street, Suite 700
San Francisco, CA 94111
(415) 392-7500 Diversified

San Joaquin Capital Corporation
Chester Troudy, President
1415 18th Street, Suite 306
Mail: P.O. Box 2538
Bakersfield, CA 93301
(805) 323-7581

Seaport Ventures, Inc.
Michael Stopler, President
525 B Street, Suite 630
San Diego, CA 92101
(619) 232-4069

Union Venture Corp.
Jeffrey Watts, President
445 South Figueroa Street
Los Angeles, CA 90071
(213) 236--4092 Diversified

VK Capital Company
Franklin Van Kasper, General Partner
50 California Street, Suite 202
San Francisco, CA 94111
(415) 391-5600 Diversified

Vista Capital Corp.
Frederick J. Howden, Jr., Chairman
5080 Shoreham Place, Suite 202
San Diego, CA 92122
(619) 453-0780 Diversified

Walden Capital Partners
Arthur S. Berliner, President
750 Battery Street, Seventh Floor
San Francisco, CA 94111
(415) 391-7225 Diversified

Westamco Investment Company
Leonard G. Muskin, President
8929 Wilshire Blvd., Suite 400
Beverly Hills, CA 90211
(213) 652-8288 66 percent Real Estate

Colorado

Associated Capital Corporation
Rodney J. Love, President
4891 Independence Street, Suite 201

Wheat Ridge, CO 80033
(303) 420-8155 Grocery Stores

UBD Capital Inc.
Allan R. Haworth, President
1700 Broadway
Denver, CO 80274
(303) 863-6329 Diversified

Connecticut

AB SBIC, Inc.
Adam J. Bozzuto, President
275 School House Road
Cheshire, CT 06410
(203) 272-0203 Grocery Stores

All State Venture Capital Corporation
Ceasar N. Anquillare, President
The Bishop House
32 Elm Street, P.O. Box 1629
New Haven, CT 06506
(203) 787-5029 Diversified

Capital Impact Corp.
William D. Starbuck, President
961 Main Street
Bridgeport, CT 06601
(203) 384-5670 Diversified

Capital Resource Co. of Connecticut
I. Martin Fierberg, Managing Partner
699 Bloomfield Avenue
Bloomfield, CT 06002
(203) 243-1114 Diversified

Dewey Investment Corp.
George E. Mrosek, President
101 Middle Turnpike West
Manchester, Ct 06040
(203) 649-0654 Diversified

First Connecticut SBIC
David Engelson, President
177 State Street
Bridgeport, CT 06604
(203) 366-4726 50 percent Real Estate

First New England Capital, LP
Richard C. Klaffky, President
255 Main Street
Hartford, CT 06106
(203) 249-4321 Diversified

Marcon Capital Corp.
Martin A. Cohen, President
49 Riverside Avenue
Westport, CT 06880
(203)226-6893 Diversified

Northeastern Capital Corporation
Joseph V. Ciaburri, Chairman and CEO
209 Church Street
New Haven, CT 06510
(203) 865-4500 Diversified

Regional Financial Enterprises, L.P.
Robert M. Williams, Managing Partner
36 Grove Street
New Canaan, CT 06840
203) 367-3282   Diversified

SBIC of Connecticut Inc.
Kenneth F. Zarrilli, President
1115 Main Street
Bridgeport, CT 06603
(203) 367-3282   Diversified

Deleware
Morgan Investment Corporation
William E. Pike, Chairman
902 Market Street
Wilmington, DE 19801
(302) 651-2500 Diversified

District Of Columbia
Allied Investment Corporation
David J. Gladstone, President
1666 K Street, N.W. Suite 901
Washington, DC 20006
(202) 331-1112 Diversified

American Security Capital Corp., Inc.
William G. Tull, President
730 Fifteenth Street, N.W.
Washington, DC 20013
(202) 624-4843 Diversified

DC Bancorp Venture Capital Company
Allan A. Weissburg, President
1801 K Street, N.W.
Washington, DC 20006
(202) 955-6970 Diversified

Washington Ventures, Inc.
Kenneth A. Swain, President
1320 18th Street, N.W.
Suite 300
Washington, DC 20036
(202) 895-2560 Diversified

Florida
Allied Investment Corporation
(Main Office: Washington, DC)
Executive Office Center, Suite 305
2770 N. Indian River Blvd.
Vero Beach, FL 32960
(407) 778-5556

Caribank Capital Corp
Michael E. Chaney, President
2400 East Commercial Boulevard
Suite 814
Fort Lauderdale, FL 33308
(305) 776-1133 Diversified

First North Florida SBIC
J.B. Higdon, President
1400 Gadsden Street
P.O. Box 1021
Quincy, FL 32351
(904) 875-2600 Grocery Stores

Gold Coast Capital Corporation
William I. Gold, President
3550 Biscayne Blvd., Room 601
Miami, FL 33137
(305) 576-2012 Diversified

J & D Capital Corp.
Jack Carmel, President
12747 Biscayne Blvd.
North Miami, FL 33181
(305) 893-0303 Diversified

Market Capital Corp.
E. E. Eads, President
1102 North 28th Street
P.O. Box 22667
Tampa, FL 33630
(813) 247-1357 Grocery Stores

Southeast Venture Capital Limited
James R. Fitzsimons, Jr, President
3250 Miami Center
100 Chopin Plaza
Miami, FL 33131
(305) 379-2005 Diversified

Western Financial Capital Corporation
Dr. F. M. Rosemore, President

1380 N. E. Miami Gardens Drive
Suite 225
N. Miami Beach, FL 33179
(305) 949-5900 Medical

Georgia
Investor's Equity, Inc.
Walter Fisher, President
2629 First National Bank Tower
Atlanta, GA 30383
(404) 523-3999 Diversified

North Riverside Capital Corporation
Tom Barry, President
50 Technology Park/Atlanta
Norcross, GA 30092
(404) 446-5556 Diversified

Hawaii
Bancorp Hawaii SBIC
James D. Evans, Jr., President
111 South King Street
Suite 1060
Honolulu, HI 96813
(808) 521-6411 Diversified

Illinois
ANB Venture Corporation
Kurt L. Liljedahl, Exec. Vice-President
33 North LaSalle Street
Chicago, IL 60690
(312) 855-1554 Diversified

Alpha Capital Venture Partners
Andrew H. Kalnow, General Partner
Three First National Plaza, 14th Floor
Chicago, IL 60602
(312) 372-1556 Diversified

Business Ventures Incorporated

Milton Lefton, President
20 North Wacker Drive, Suite 550
Chicago, IL 60602
(312) 346-1580 Diversified

Continental Illinois Venture Corp.
John L. Hines, President
209 South LaSalle Street
Mail: 231 South LaSalle Street
Chicago, IL 60693
(312) 828-8023 Diversified

First Capital Corp. of Chicago
John A. Canning, Jr., President
Three First National Plaza
Suite 1330
Chicago, IL 60670
(312) 732-5400 Diversified

Frontenac Capital Corporation
David A. R. Dullum, President
208 South LaSalle Street, Room 1900
Chicago, IL 60604
(312) 368-0047 Diversified

LaSalle Street Capitla Corporation
Robert E. Koe, President
200 North La Salle Street
10th Floor
Chicago, IL 60601
(312) 621-7057 Diversified

Mesirow Capital Partners SBIC, Ltd.
Lester A. Morris, General Partner
350 North Clark Street
3rd Floor
Chicago, IL 60610
(312) 670-6098 Diversified

Walnut Capital Corp.
Burton W. Kanter, Chairman of the Board
208 South LaSalle Street
Chicago, IL 60604

(312) 346-2033

Indiana
1st Source Capital Corporation
Eugene L. Cavanaugh, Jr., Vice President
100 North Michigan Street
Mail: P.O. Box 1602; South Bend 46634
South Bend, IN 46601
(219) 236-2180 Diversified

Circle Ventures, Inc.
Robert Salyers, President
2502 Roosevelt Avenue
Indianapolis, IN 46218
(317) 636-7242 Diversified

Equity Resource Company, Inc.
Michael J. Hammes, Vice President
One Plaza Place
202 South Michigan Street
South Bend, IN 46601
(219) 237-5255 Diversified

Raffensperger Hughes Venture Corp.
Samuel B. Sutphin, President
20 North Meridian Street
Indianapolis, IN 46204
(317) 635-4551 Diversified

White River Capital Corporation
Thomas D. Washburn, President
500 Washington Street
Mail: P.O. Box 929
Columbus, IN 47201
(812) 372-0111 Diversified

Iowa
MorAmerica Capital Corporation
Donald E. Flynn, President
Suite 200, American Building
Cedar Rapids, IA 52401

(319) 363-8247 Diversified

Kansas
Kansas Venture Capital, Inc.
Larry J. High, President
1030 First National Bank
One Townsite Plaza
Topeka, KS 66603
(913) 235-3437 Diversified

Kentucky
Financial Opportunities, Inc.
Gary Duerr, Manager
6060 Dutchman's Lane
Mail" P.O. Box 35710; Louisville, KY 40232
Louisville, KY 40205
(502) 451-3800 Diversified

Mountain Ventures, Inc.
Roger E. Whitehouse, President
911 North Main Street
Mail: P.O. Box 628
London, KY 40741
(606) 864-5175 Diversified

Wilbur Venture Capital Corp.
(Main Office: Tucson, AZ)
400 Fincastle Building
3rd & Broadway
Louisville, KY 40202
(502) 585-1214

Louisiana
Capital Equity Corp.
Arthur J. Mitchell, General Manager
1885 Wooddale Blvd., Suite 210
Baton Rouge, LA 70806
(504) 924-9209 Diversified

Capital for Terrebonne, Inc.
Hartwell A. Lewis, President
27 Austin Drive
Houma, LA 70360
(504) 868-3930 Diversified

Dixie Business Investment Company
George Lensing, Chairman
401 - 1/2 Lake Street
P.O. Box 588
Lake Providence, LA 71254
(318) 559-1588 Diversified

Louisiana Equity Capital Corporation
G. Lee Griffin, President
451 Florida Street
Baton Rouge, LA 70821
(504) 389-4421

Maine
Maine Capital Corp.
David M. Coit, President
Seventy Center Street
Portland, ME 04101
(207) 772-1001

Maryland
First Maryland Capital, Inc.
Joseph A. Kenary, President
107 West Jefferson Street
Rockville, MD 20850
(301) 251-6630

Greater Washington Investments, Inc.
Don A. Christensen, President
5454 Wisconsin Avenue
Chevy Chase, MD 20815
(301) 656-0626

Jiffy Lube Capital Corporation
Eleanor C. Harding, President
6000 Metro Drive
Mail: P.O. Box 17223; Baltimore 21203-7223
Baltimore, MD 21215
(301) 764-3234

Massachusetts
Advent Atlantic Capital Company
David D. Croll, Managing Partner
45 Milk Street
Boston, MA 02109
(617) 338-0800

Atlas II Capital Corporation
Joost E. Tjaden, President
260 Franklin Street, Suite 1501
Boston, MA 02109
(617) 439-6160

BancBoston Ventures, Incorporated
Paul F. Hogan, President
100 Federal Street
Mail: P.O. Box 2016
Boston, MA 02106
(617) 434-2441

Bever Capital Corp.
Joost E. Tjaden, President
260 Franklin Street, 15th Floor
Boston, MA 02109
(617) 439-6160

Boston Hambro Capital Company
Edwin Goodman, President of Corp.
160 State Street, 9th Floor
Boston, MA 02109
(617) 523-7767

Business Achievement Corporation
Michael L. Katzeff, President

1172 Beacon Street, Suite 202
Newton, MA 02161
(617) 965-0550

Chestnut Capital International
David D. Croll, Managing Partner
45 Milk Street
Boston, MA 02109
(617) 338-0800

First Capital Corp. of Chicago
(Main Office: Chicago, IL)
133 Federal Street, 6th Floor
Boston, MA 02110
(617) 542-9185

First United SBIC, Inc.
Alfred W. Ferrara, Vice President
135 Will Drive
Canton, MA 02021
(617) 828-6150

Fleet Venture Resources, Inc.
(Main Office: Providence, RI)
Carlton V. Klein, Vice-President
60 State Street
Boston, MA 02109
(617) 367-6700

Mezzanine Capital Corporation
David D. Croll, President
45 Milk Street
Boston, MA 02109
(617) 574-6752

Milk Street Partners, Inc.
Richard H. Churchill, Jr., President
45 Milk Street
Boston, MA 02109
(617) 574-6723

Monarch - Narrangansett Ventures, Inc.
George W. Siguler, President

One Financial Plaza
Springfield, MA 01102
(413) 781-3000

New England Capital Corporation
Z. David Patterson, Vice President
One Washington Mall, 7th Floor
Boston, MA 02108
(617) 722-6400

Northeast SBI Corp.
Joseph Mindick, Treasurer
16 Cumberland Street
Boston, MA 02115
(617) 267-3983

Orange Nassau Capital Corporation
Joost E. Tjaden, President
260 Franklin Street, 15th Floor
Boston, MA 02109
(617) 742-7825

Shawmut National Capital Corporation
William L.G. Lester, President
c/o Shawmut Bank N.A.
One Federal Street
Boston, MA 02210
(617) 292-4128

Stevens Capital Corporation
Edward Capuano, President
168 Stevens Street
Fall River, MA 02721
(617) 679-0044

UST Capital Corp.
Walter Dick, President
40 Court Street
Boston, MA 02108
(617) 726-7137

Vadus Capital Corp.
Joost E. Tjaden, President

260 Franklin Street, 15th Floor
Boston, MA 02109
(617) 439-6160

Michigan
Doan Resources Limited Partnership
Herbert D. Doan, Partner
4251 Plymouth Road
P.O. Box 986
Ann Arbor, MI 48106
(313) 747-9401

Michigan Tech Capital Corporation
Clark L. Pellegrini, President
Technology Park
601 West Sharon Avenue; P.O. Box 364
Houghton, MI 49931
(906) 487-2970

Minnesota
FBS SBIC, Limited Partnership
Dennis E. Evans, President
1100 First Bank Place East
Minneapolis, MN 55480
(612) 370-4764

Hidden Oaks Financial Services, Inc.
C. Patrick Schulke, President
4620 West 77th Street, Suite 155
Edina, MN 55435
(612) 897-3902

Itasca Growth Fund, Inc.
Carroll Bergerson, General Manager
One N.W. Third Street
Grand Rapids, MN 55744
(218) 327-6200

North Star Ventures Inc.
Terrence W. Glarner, President

100 South Fifth Street
Suite 2200
Minneapolis, MN 55402
(612) 333-1133

Northland Capital Venture Partnership
George G. Barnum, Jr., President
613 Missabe Building
Duluth, MN 55802
(218) 722-0545

Northwest Venture Partners
Robert F. Zicarelli, Managing G.P.
2800 Piper Jaffray Tower
222 South Ninth Street
Minneapolis, MN 55402
(612) 372-8770

Norwest Growth Fund, Inc.
Daniel J. Haggerty, President
2800 Piper Jaffray Tower
222 South Ninth Street
MInneapolis, MN 55402
(612) 372-8770

Shared Ventures, Inc.
Howard W. Weiner, President
6550 York Avenue South
Suite 419
Edina, MN 55435
(612) 925-3411

Mississippi
Vicksburg SBIC
David L. May, President
302 First National Bank Building
Vicksburg, MS 39180
(601) 636-4762

Missouri
Bankers Capital Corp.

Raymond E. Glasnapp, President
3100 Gillham Road
Kansas City, MO 64109
(816) 531-1600

Capital For Business, Inc.
James B. Hebenstreit, President
1000 Walnut, 18th Floor
Kansas City, MO 64106
(816) 234-2357

Capital for Business, Inc.
(Main Office: Kansas City, MO)
11 South Meramec, Suite 804
St. Louis, MO 63105
(816) 471-1700

MorAmerica Capital Corporation
(Main Office: Cedar Rapids, IA)
911 Main Street, Suite 2724A
Commerce Tower Building
Kansas City, MO 64105
(816) 842-0114

United Missouri Capital Corporation
Joe Kessinger, Manager
1010 Grand Avenue
Kansas City, MO 64106
Mail: P.O. Box 419226; K.C., MO 64141
(816) 556-7333

Nebraska
United Financial Resources Corp.
Dennis L. Schulte, Manager
6211 L. Street
Mail: P.O. Box 1131
Omaha, NE 68101
(402) 734-1250

Nevada
Enterprise Finance Capital Development Corp.

167

Robert N. Hampton, President
First Interstate Bank of Nevada Bldg.
One East First Street, Suite 1100
Reno, NV 89501
(702) 329-7797

New Hampshire
VenCap, Inc.
Richard J. Ash, President
1155 Elm Street
Manchester, NH 03101
(603) 644-6100

New Jersey
Bishop Capital, L.P.
Charles J. Irish
58 Park Place
Newark, NJ 07102
(201) 623-0171

ESLO Capital Corp.
Leo Katz, President
212 Wright Street
Newark, NJ 07114
(201) 242-4488

First Princeton Capital Corporation
Michael D. Feinstein, President
Five Garret Mountain Plaza
West Paterson, NJ 07424
(201) 278-8111

Monmouth Capital Corp.
Eugene W. Landy, President
125 Wycoff Road
Midland National Bank Bldg. -P.O. Box 335
Eatontown, NJ 07724
(201) 542-1927

Tappan Zee Capital Corporation
Karl Kirschner, President

201 Lower Notch Road
Little Falls, NJ 07424
(201) 256-8280

Unicorn Ventures
Frank P. Diassi, General Partner
6 Commerce Drive
Cranford, NJ 07016
(201) 276-7880

United Jersey Venture Capital, Inc.
Stephen H. Paneyko, President
301 Carnegie Center
P.O. Box 2066
Princeton, NJ 08540
(609) 987-3490

New Mexico
Albuquerque SBIC
Albert T. Ussery, President
501 Tijeras Avenue, N.W.
P.O. Box 487
Albuquerque, NM 87103
(505) 247-0145

Equity Capital Corp.
Jerry A. Henson, President
119 East Marcy Street, Suite 101
Santa Fe, NM 87501
(505) 988-4273

Southwest Capital Investments, Inc.
Martin J. Roe, President
The Southwest Building
3500-E Comanche Road, N.E.
Albuquerque, NM 87107
(505) 884-7161

United Mercantile Capital Corp.
Joe Justice, General Manager
2400 Louisiana Blvd., Bldg. 4, Suite 101
Albuquerque, NM 87110

Mail: P.O. Box 37487 Albuquerque 87176
(505) 883-7776

New York
767 Limited Partnership
H. Wertheim and H. Mallement, G.P.
767 Third Avenue
New York, NY 10017
(212) 838-7776

ASEA - Harvest partners
Harvey Wertheim, General Partner
767 Third Avenue
New York, NY10017
(212) 838-7776

American Commercial Capital Corporation
Gerald J. Grossman, President
310 Madison Avenue, Suite 1304
New York, NY 10017
(212) 986-3305

American Energy Investment Corp.
John J. Hoey, Chairman of the Board
645 Fifth Avenue, Suite 1900
New York, NY 10022
(212) 688-7307 Energy Industries

Amev Capital Corp.
Martin Orland, President
One World Trade Center
50th Floor
New York, NY 10048
(212) 832-1104

BT Capital Corp.
James G. Hellmuth, President
280 Park Avenue - 10 West
New York, NY 10017
(212) 850-1916

Boston Hambro Capital Company
(Main Office: Boston, MA)
17 East 71st Street
New York, NY 10022
(212) 888-4004

CMNY Capital
Robert Davidoff, General Partner
77 Water Street
New York, NY 10005
(212) 437-7078

Central New York SBIC
Robert E. Romig, President
351 South Warren Street
Syracuse, NY 13202
(315) 478-5026 Vending Machine

Chase Manhattan Capital Corporation
Gustav H. Koven, President
1 Chase Manhattan Plaza - 23rd Floor
New York, NY 10081
(212) 552-6275

Chemical Venture Capital Associates
Steven J. Gilbert, President
277 Park Avenue, 10th Floor
New York, NY 10043
(212) 310-7578

Citicorp Venture Capital, Ltd.
William Comfort, Chairman of the Board
153 East 53rd Street, 28th Floor
New York, NY 10043
(212) 559-1127

Clinton Capital Corp.
Mark Scharfman, President
79 Madison Avenue, Suite 800
New York, NY 10016
(212) 696-4334

Croyden Capital Corp.
Lawrence D. Garfinkle, President
45 Rockefeller Plaza, Suite 2165
New York, NY 10111
(212) 974-0184

Diamond Capital Corp.
Steven B. Kraiety, President
805 Third Avenue, Suite 1100
New York, NY 1001i7
(212) 838-1255

EAB Venture Corp.
Mark R. Littell, President
EAB Plaza
Uniondale, NY 11555
(516) 296-5784

Edwards Capital Company
Edward H. Teitlebaum, President
215 Lexington Avenue, Suite 805
New York, NY 10016
(212) 686-2568

Fairfield Equity Corp.
Matthew A. Berdon, President
200 East 42nd Street
New York, NY 10017
(212) 867-0150

Ferranti High Technology, Inc.
Sandford R. Simon, President & Director
515 Madison Avenue
New York, NY 10022
(212) 688-9828

Fifty-Third Street Ventures
Patricia Cloherty & Dan Tessler
155 Main Street
Cold Spring, NY 10516
(914) 265-5167

First New York SBIC
Israel Mindick, General Partner
20 Squadron Blvd., Suite 480
New City, NY 10956
(914) 638-1550

Franklin Corp. (The)
Norman S. Strobel, President
767 Fifth Avenue
G.M. Building, 23rd Floor
New York, NY 10153
(212) 486-2323

Fundex Capital Corp.
Howard Sommer, President
525 Northern Blvd.
Great Neck, NY 11021
(516) 466-8551

GHW Capital Corp.
Nesta Stephens, V.P. & Administrator
489 Fifth Avenue
New York, NY 10017
(212) 687-1708

Genesee Funding, Inc.
A. Keene Bolton, President, CEO
100 Corporate Woods
Rochester, NY 14623
(716) 272-2332

Hanover Capital Corp.
Geoffrey T. Selzer, President
150 East 58th Street, Suite 2710
New York, NY 10155
(212) 980-9670

Intergroup Venture Capital Corp.
Ben Hauben, President
230 Park Avenue
New York, NY 10017
(212) 661-5428

Interstate Capital Company, Inc.
David Scharf, President
380 Lexington Avenue
New York, NY 10017
(212) 986-7333

Irving Capital Corp.
Andrew McWethy, President
1290 Avenue of the Americas
New York, NY 10104
(212) 408-4800

Kwiat Capital Corp.
Sheldon F. Kwiat, President
576 Fifth Avenue
New York, NY 10036
(212) 391-2461

M & T Capital Corp.
William Randon, President
One M & T Plaza
Buffalo, NY 14240
(716) 842-5881

MH Capital Investors, Inc.
Edward L. Kock III, President
270 Park Avenue
New York, NY 10017
(212) 286-3222

Multi-Purpose Capital Corporation
Eli B. Fine, President
31 South Broadway
Yonkers, NY 10701
(914) 963-2733

NYBDC Capital Corp.
Robert W. Lazar, President
41 State Street
Albany, NY 12207
(518) 463-2268

NYSTRS/NV Capital Limited Partnership
Raymond A. Lancaster, President
One Norstar Plaza
Albany, NY 12207
(518) 447-4050

NatWest USA Capital Corporation
Orville G. Aarons, General Manager
175 Water Street
New York, NY 10038
(212) 602-1200

Nelson Capital Corp.
Irwin Nelson, President
585 Stewart Avenue, Suite 416
Garden City, L.I., NY 11530
(516) 222-2555

Norstar Capital Inc.
Raymond A. Lancaster, President
One Norstar Plaza
Albany, NY 12207
(518) 447-4043

Onondaga Venture Capital Fund, Inc.
Irving W. Schwartz, Exec. V.P.
327 State Tower Building
Syracuse, NY 13202
(315) 478-0157

Preferential Capital Corporation
Bruce Bayroff, Secretary-Treasurer
16 Court Street
Brooklyn, NY 11241
(718) 855-2728

Pyramid Ventures, Inc.
John Popovitch, Treasurer
280 Park Avenue
New York, NY 10015
(212) 850-1934

Questech Capital Corp.
John E. Koonce, President
320 Park Avenue, 3rd Floor
New York, NY 10022
(212) 891-7500

R & R Financial Corp.
Imre Rosenthal, President
1451 Broadway
New York, NY 10036
(212) 790-1441

Rand SBIC, Inc.
Donald Ross, President
1300 Rand Building
Buffalo, NY 14203
(716) 853-0802

Realty Growth Capital Corporation
Lawrence Beneson, President
331 Madison Avenue
Fourth Floor East
New York, NY 10017
(212) 661-8380   100% Real Estate Specialist

Republic SBI Corporation
Robert V. Treanor, Senior V.P.
452 Fifth Avenue
New York, NY 10018
(212) 930-8639

SLK Capital Corp.
Edward A. Kerbs, President
115 Broadway, 20th Floor
New York, NY 10006
(212) 587-8800

Small Bus. Electronics Investment Corp.
Stanley Meisels, President
1220 Peninsula Blvd.
Hewlett, NY 11557
(516) 374-0743

Southern Tier Capital Corporation
Harold Gold, Secretary - Treasurer
55 South Main Street
Liberty, NY 12754
(914) 292-3030

TLC Funding Corp.
Philip G. Kass, President
141 South Central Avenue
Hartsdale, NY 10530
(914) 683-1144

Tappan Zee Capital Corporation
(Main Office: Little Falls, NJ)
120 North Main Street
New City, NY 10956
(914) 634-8890

Telesciences Capital Corporation
Mike A. Petrozzo, Contact
26 Broadway, Suite 841
New York, NY 10004
(212) 425-0320

Vega Capital Corp.
Victor Harz, President
720 White Plains Road
Scarsdale, NY 10583
(914) 472-8550

Venture SBIC, Inc.
Arnold Feldman, President
249-12 Jericho Turnpike
Floral Park, NY 11001
(516) 352-0068

WFG-Harvest Partners, Ltd.
Harvey J. Wertheim, General Partner
767 Third Avenue
New York, NY 10017
(212) 838-7776

Winfield Capital Corp.
Stanley M. Pechman, President
237 Mamaroneck Avenue
White Plains, NY 10605
(914) 949-2600

Wood River Capital Corporation
Elizabeth W. Smith, President
645 Madison Avenue
New York, NY 10022
(212) 750-9420

North Carolina
Delta Capital, Inc.
Alex B. Wilkins, Jr., President
227 North Tryon Street, Suite 201
Charlotte, NC 28202
(704) 372-1410

Falcon Capital Corp.
P.S. Prasad, President
400 West Fifth Street
Greenville, NC 27834
(919) 752-5918

Heritage Capital Corp.
William R. Starnes, President
2095 Two First Union Plaza
Charlotte, NC 28282
(704) 334-2867 50 percent Real Estate

Kitty Hawk Capital, Limited Partnership
Walter H. Wilkinson, President
Independence Center, Suite 1640
Charlotte, NC 28246
(704) 333-3777

NCNB SBIC Corporation
Troy S. McCrory, Jr., President
One NCNB Plaza - TO5 - 2
Charlotte, NC 28255
(704) 374-5583

NCNB Venture Company
S. Epes Robinson, General Partner
One NCNB Plaza, T-39
Charlotte, NC 28255
(704) 374-5723

Ohio
A.T. Capital Corp.
Robert C. Salipante, President
900 Euclid Avenue, T-18
Mail: P.O. Box 5937

Cleveland, OH 44101
(216) 687-4970

Banc One Capital Corporation
James E. Kolls, Vice President
100 East Broad Street
Columbus, OH 43215
(614) 248-5932

Capital Funds Corp.
Carl G. Nelson, Chief Inv. Officer
800 Superior Avenue
Cleveland, OH 44114

Clarion Capital Corp.
Morton A. Cohen, President
35555 Curtis Blvd.
Eastlake, OH 44094
(216) 953-0555

First Ohio Capital Corporation
David J. McMacken, General Manager
606 Madison Avenue
Toledo, OH 43604
(419) 259-7146
Mail: P.O. Box 2061; Toledo, OH 43603

Gries Investment Company
Robert D. Gries, President
1500 Statler Office Tower
Cleveland, OH 44115
(216) 861-1146

JRM Capital Corp.
H.F. Meyer, President
110 West Streetsboro Street
Hudson, OH 44236
(216) 656-4010

National City Capital Corporation
Michael Sherwin, President
629 Euclid Avenue
Cleveland, OH 44114

(216) 575-2491

River Capital Corporation
(Main Office: Alexandria, VA)
796 Huntington Building
Cleveland, OH 44114
(216) 781-3655

SeaGate Venture Management, Inc.
Charles A. Brown, Vice-President
245 Summit Street, Suite 1403
Toledo, OH 43603
(419) 259-8605

Tamco Investors Incorporated
Nathan H. Monus, President
375 Victoria Road
Youngstown, OH 44515
(216) 792-3811

Oklahoma
Alliance Business Investment Company
Barry Davis, President
17 East Second Street
One Williams Center, Suite 2000
Tulsa, OK 74172
(918) 584-3581

Western Venture Capital Corporation
William B. Baker, Chief Operating Officer
4880 South Lewis
Tulsa, OK 74105
(918) 749-7981

Oregon
First Interstate Capital, Inc.
(Main Office: Newport Beach, CA)
227 S.W. Pine Street, Suite 200
Portland, OR 97204
(503) 223-4334

Northern Pacific Capital Corporation
John J. Tennant, JR., President
1201 S.W. 12th Avenue, Suite 608
Portland, OR 97205
Mail: P.O. Box 1658; Portland, OR 97207

Norwest Growth Fund, Inc.
(Main Office: Minneapolis, MN)
1300 S.W. 5th Street, Suite 3108
Portland, OR 97201
(503) 223-6622

Pennsylvania

Capital Corporation of America
Martin M. Newman, President
225 South 15th Street, Suite 920
Philadelphia, PA 19102
(215) 732-1666

Enterprise Venture Capital
Corporation of Pennsylvania
Don Cowie, C.E.O.
227 Franklin Street, Suite 215
Johnstown, PA 15901
(814) 535-7597

Erie SBIC
George R. Heaton, President
32 West 8th Street, Suite 615
Erie, PA 16501
(814) 453-7964

Fidelcor Capital Corporation
Bruce H. Luehrs, President
123 S. Broad Street
Philadelphia, PA 19109
(215) 985-7287

First SBIC of California
(Main Office: Costa Mesa, CA)
Daniel A. Dye, Contact
P.O. Box 512

Washington, PA 15301
(412) 223-0707

First Valley Capital Corporation
Matthew W. Thomas, President
640 Hamilton Mall, 8th Floor
Allentown, PA 18101
(215) 776-6760

Franklin Corp.
(Main Office: New York, NY)
Plymouth Meeting Executive Congress
Suite 461-610 W. Germantown Pike
Plymouth Meeting, PA 19462

Meridian Capital Corp.
Joseph E. Laky, President
Suite 222, Blue Bell West
650 Skippack Pike
Blue Bell, PA 19422
(215) 278-8907

Meridian Venture Partners
Raymond R. Rafferty, General Partner
The Fidelity Court Building
259 Radnor-Chester Road
Radnor, PA 19087
(215) 293-0210

PNC Capital Corp.
Gary J. Zentner, President
Pittsburgh National Building
Fifth Avenue and Wood Street
Pittsburgh, PA 15222
(412) 355-2245

Rhode Island
Domestic Capital Corp.
Nathaniel B. Baker, President
815 Reservoir Avenue
Cranston, RI 02910
(401) 946-3310

Fleet Venture Resources, Inc.
Robert M. Van Degna, President
111 Westminster Street
Providence, RI 02903
(401) 278-6770

Moneta Capital Corp.
Arnold Kilberg, President
285 Governor Street
Providence, RI 02906
(401) 861-4600

Old Stone Capital Corporation
Arthur C. Barton, President
One Old Stone Square, 11th Floor
Providence, RI 02903
(401) 278-2559

River Capital Corporation
(Main Office: Alexandria, VA)
555 South Main Street
Providence, RI 02903
(401) 861-7470

Wallace Capital Corporation
Lloyd W. Granoff, President
170 Westminster Street
Suite 300
Providence, RI 02903
(401) 273-9191

South Carolina
Carolina Venture Cap. Corporation
Thomas H. Harvey III, President
14 Archer Road
Hilton Head Isl., SC 29928
(803) 842-3101

Charleston Capital Corporation
Henry Yaschick, President
111 Church Street

P.O. Box 328
Charleston, SC 29402
(803) 723-6464

Floco Investment Company, Inc.
William H. Johnson, Sr., President
Highway 52 North
Scranton, SC 29561
(803) 389-2731

Lowcountry Investment Corporation
Joseph T. Newton, Jr., President
4444 Daley Street
P.O. Box 10447
Charleston, SC 29411
(803) 554-9880   Grocery Stores

Reedy River Ventures
John M. Sterling, President
400 Haywood Road
Greenville, SC 29606
(803) 297-9198
Mail: P.O. Box 17526

Tennessee
Financial Resources, Incorporated
Milton Picard, Chairman of the Board
2800 Sterick Building
Memphis, TN 38101
(901) 578-2405

Texas
Alliance Business Investment Company
(Main Office: Tulsa, OK)
911 Louisiana
One Shell Plaza, Suite 3990
Houston, TX 77002
(713) 224-8224

Americap Corporation
James L. Hurn, President

7575 San Felipe
Houston, TX 77063
(713) 780-8084

Ameriway Venture Partners I
James L. Hurn, General Partner
7575 San Felipe
Houston, TX 77063
(713) 780-8084

Brittany Capital Company
Steve Peden, Partner
1525 Elm Street
2424 LTV Tower
Dallas, TX 75201
(214) 954-1515

Business Capital Corp.
James E. Sowell, Chairman of the Board
4809 Cole Avenue, Suite 250
Dallas, TX 75205
(214) 522-3739

Capital Marketing Corporation
Ray Ballard, Manager
100 Nat Gibbs Drive
P.O. Box 1000
Keller, TX 76248
(817) 656-7309 Grocery Stores

Capital Southwest Venture Corp.
William R. Thomas, President
12900 Presotn Road, Suite 700
Dallas, TX 75230
(214) 233-8242

Central Texas SBI Corporation
David G. Horner, President
P.O. Box 2600
Waco, TX 76702
(817) 753-6461

Charter Venture Group, Incorporated
Winston C. Davis, President
2600 Citadel Plaza Drive, Suite 600
Houston, TX 77008
(713) 863-0704

Citicorp Venture Capital, Ltd.
(Main Office: New York, NY)
717 North Harwood Street
Dallas, TX 75201
(214) 880-9670

Energy Assets, Inc.
Laurence E. Simmons, Exec. V.P.
4900 Republic Bank Center
700 Louisiana
Houston, TX 77002
(713) 236-9999

Enterprise Capital Corporation
Fred Zeidman, President
4543 Post Oak Place, #130
Houston, TX 77027
(713) 621-9444

FCA Investment Company
Robert S. Baker, Chairman
3000 Post Oak, Suite 1790
Houston, TX 77056
(713) 965-0061

First Interstate Capital Corporation of Texas
Richard S. Smith, President
1000 Louisiana, 7th Floor
Houston, TX 77002
Mail: P.O. Box 3326; Houston, TX 77253
(713) 224-6611

Ford Capital, Ltd.
C. Jeff Pan, President
1525 Elm Street
Dallas, TX 75201

Mail: P.O. Box 2140; Dallas TX 75221

MCap Corp.
J. Wayne Gaylord, Manager
1717 Main Street, 6th Floor
Momentum Place
Dallas, TX 75201
(214) 939-3131

MVenture Corp.
Wayne Gaylord, Sr., Vice-President
1717 Main Street, 6th Fl -Momentum Place
Dallas, TX 75201
Mail: P.O. Box 662090; Dallas, TX 75266
(214) 939-3131

Mapleleaf Capital Ltd.
Edward Fink, President
55 Waugh, Suite 710
Houston, TX 77007
(713) 880-4494

Mid-State Capital Corporation
Smith E. Thomasson, President
510 North Valley Mills Drive
Waco, TX 76710
(817) 772-9220

Neptune Capital Corporation
Richard C. Strauss, President
5956 Sherry Lane, Suite 800
Dallas, TX 75225
(214) 739-1414

North Riverside Capital Corporation
(Main Office: Atlanta, GA)
400 North St. Paul, Suite 1265
Dallas, TX 75201
(214) 220-2717

Omega Capital Corporation
Theodric E. Moor, Jr., President
755 South 11th Street, Suite 250

Beaumont, TX 77704
Mail: P.O. Box 2173
(409) 832-0221

Republic Venture Group Incorporated
Robert H. Wellborn, Pres. & General Mgr.
325 N. St. Paul 2829 Tower 11
Dallas, TX 75201
Mail: P.O. Box 655961; Dallas, TX 75265
(214) 922-3500

Revelation Resources, Ltd.
Mr. Chris J. Mathews, Manager
2929 Allen Parkway, Suite 1705
Houston, TX 77019
(713) 526-5623

Rust Capital Limited
Jeffrey Garvey, Partner
114 West 7th Street, Suite 500
Austin, TX 78701
(512) 482-0806

SBI Capital Corp.
William E. Wright, President
6305 Beverly Hill Lane
Houston TX 77057
Mail: P.O. Box 570368; Houston, TX 77257
(713) 975-1188

San Antonio Venture Group, Inc.
Domingo Bueno, President
2300 West Commerce Street
San Antonio, TX 78207
(512) 573-5151

Southwestern Venture Capital of Texas, Inc.
James A. Bettersworth, President
1336 East Court Street
P.O. Box 1719
Seguin, TX 78155
(512) 379-0380

Southwestern Venture Cap. of Texas, Inc.
(Main Office: Seguin, TX)
1250 N.E. Loop 410, Suite 300
San Antonio, TX 78209
(512) 822-9949

Sunwestern Capital Corporation
Thomas W. Wright, President
3 Forest Plaza
12221 Merit Drive, Suite 1300
Dallas, TX 75251
(214) 239-5650

Sunwestern Ventures Company
Thomas W. Wright, President
3 Forest Plaza
12221 Merit Drive, Suite 1300
Dallas, TX 75251
(214) 239-5650

Texas Commerce Investment Company
Fred Lummis, Vice President
Texas Commerce Bank Bldg., 30th Floor
712 Main Street
Houston, TX 77002
(713) 236-4719

Wesbanc Ventures, Ltd.
Stuart Schube, General Partner
2401 Fountanview, Suite 950
Houston, TX 77057
(713) 977-7421

Vermont
Queneska Capital Corporation
Albert W. Coffrin, III, President
123 Church Street
Burlington, VT 05401
(802) 865-1806

Virginia
Crestar Capital
A. Hugh Ewing, III, Managing G.P.
9 South 12th Street - Third Floor
Richmond, VA 23219
(804) 643-7358

James River Capital Associates
A. Hugh Ewing, Managing Partner
9 South 12th Street
Richmond, VA 23214
Mail: P.O. Box 1776; Richmond, VA 23219
(804) 643-7323

Metropolitan Capital Corporation
John B. Toomey, President
2550 Huntington Avenue
Alexandria, VA 22303
(703) 960-4698

River Capital Corporation
Peter Van Oosterhout, President
1033 N. Fairfax Street
Alexandria, VA 22314
(703) 739-2100

Sovran Funding Corp.
David A. King, Jr., President
Sovran Center, 6th Floor
One Commercial Plaza; Mail: P.O. Box 600
Norfolk, VA 23510
(804) 441-4041

Tidewater Industrial Capital Corporation
Armand Caplan, President
Suite 1424 United Virginia Bank Building
Norfolk, VA 23510
(804) 622-1501

Tidewater SBI Corp.
Gregory H. Wingfield, President
1214 First Virginia Bank Tower

101 St. Paul's Blvd.
Norfolk, VA 23510
(804) 627-2315

Washington
Capital Resources Corporation
T. Evans Wyckoff, President
1001 Logan Building
Seattle, WA 98101
(206) 623-6550

Northwest Business Investment Corp.
C. Paul Sandifur, President
929 West Sprague Avenue
Spokane, WA 99204
(509) 838-3111

Peoples Capital Corporation
Robert E. Karns, President
1415 Fifth Avenue
Seattle, WA 98171
(206) 344-5463

Seafirst Capital Corporation
R. Bruce Harrod, President
Columbia Seafirst Center
701 Fifth Avenue, P.O. Box 34103
Seattle, WA 98124
(206) 358-7441

Washington Trust Equity Corp.
John M. Snead, President
Washington Trust Financial Center
P.O. Box 2127
Spokane, WA 99210
(509) 455-4106

Wisconsin
Bando-McGlocklin Capital Corporation
George Schonath, Investment Advisor
13555 Bishops Court, Suite 225

Brookfield, WI 53005
(414) 784-9010

Capital Investments, Inc.
Robert L. Banner, Vice President
Commerce Building, Suite 400
744 North Fourth Street
Milwaukee, WI 53203
(414) 273-6560

M & I Ventures Corp.
John T. Byrnes, President
770 North Water Street
Milwaukee, WI 53202
(414) 765-791 0

Marine Venture Capital, Inc.
H. Wayne Foreman, President
111 East Wisconsin Avenue
Milwaukee, WI 53202
(414) 765-2274

MorAmerica Capital Corporation
(Main Office: Cedar Rapids, Iowa)
600 East Mason Street
Milwaukee, WI 53202
(414) 276-3839

Super Market Investors, Inc.
David H. Maass, President
23000 Roundy Drive
Pewaukee, WI 53072
Mail: P.O. Box 473; Milwaukee 53202   Grocery Stores

Wisconsin Community Capital, Inc.
Francis J. David, General Manager
14 West Mifflin Street
Suite 314
Madison, WI 53703
(608) 256-3441

Wyoming
Capital Corporation of Wyoming, Inc.
Scott Weaver, Manager
P.O. Box 3599
145 South Durbin Street
Casper, WY 82602
(307) 234-5351

Chapter Four

Doing Business With The Government

The government has hundreds of ways to help you fund your new small business through grants, but many new business owners are not aware of the government programs aimed at helping the small businessman to deal with the government. The government realizes how vitally important small business is to our nation's economy, and therefore wants to make sure that small businesses prosper by guaranteeing them a market for their products and services. By simply filling out a few forms you can find yourself dealing with the federal government on a professional basis, and if you are a minority, handicapped, disadvantaged, or female business owner, you stand an even better chance.

Nearly every government agency needs to purchase some type of supplies. Some buy pencils and typewriters, others procure F-16 fighter jets and M-1 tanks. If every employee of the government who needed something made the purchase themselves, the accounting and record keeping paperwork would be overwhelming. Instead, all government agencies go through an office in their department called the "procurement office" which has the sole job of obtaining all the supplies and services necessary to keep the agency running. Rather than taking a trip to the local department store, however, the procurement offices keep a file of government contractors which they can draw upon to fulfill these needs. Every business on these lists has a chance to bid on the contract which the procurement office presents, and the lowest bidder will be awarded the contract.

Once the prime contract has been awarded, the contractor can choose either to fill it himself, or to sub-contract parts of it out to smaller businesses. Sub-contracting is another method by which small businesses can take advantage of government money.

Various programs of the government dictate that a certain portion of government business **must** go to small businesses. These are called "set-aside" programs, because the business is literally set-aside for small businesses to compete over. Often business will be set-aside for a special type of small business, such as veteran or minority owned businesses. If you have a small business, your opportunities with our government are great.

Federal Procurement Offices

This office offers counseling on obtaining contracts and subcontracts with the U.S. Government. It has information pertaining to "set asides" and other special programs designed to help small businesses with the U.S. government. They provide information on the latest areas of research as well natural resources and other surplus the Feds have available. For more information contact the office in Washington at the following address, or at a regional office nearest you.

Washington: Procurement Assistance,
Small Business Administration
1441 L Street NW, Room 600
Washington, D.C. 20416/ (202) 653-6635

Regional Offices:

Maine, New Hampshire, Rhode Island, Massachusetts, Vermont, Connecticut
Procurement Specialist
60 Batterymarch
10th Floor
Boston, MA 02110
617-233-3162

New York, New Jersey, Puerto Rico, Virgin Islands
Procurement Specialist
26 Federal Plaza
New York, NY 10278

212-264-7770

Pennsylvania, Maryland, West Virginia, Delaware, District of Columbia
Procurement Specialist
Suite 646-West Lobby
231 S. Asaphs Road
Bala Cynwyd, PA 19004
215-596-0172

North Carolina, South Carolina, Georgia, FLorida, Mississippi, Alabama, Kentucky, Tennessee
Procurement Specialist
1375 Peachtree ST. NE
5th Floor
Atlanta, GA 30367
404-881-7587

Ohio, Illinois, Indiana, Wisconsin, Michigan, Minnesota
Procurement Specialist
219 S. Dearborn Street
Room 858
Chicago, IL 60604
312-886-4727

Texas, Louisiana, Arkansas, Oklahoma, Michigan, Minnesota
Procurement Specialist
8625 King George Dr.
Bldg. C
Dallas, TX 7525-3391
214-767-7639

Kansas, Missouri, Nebraska, Iowa
Procurement Specialist
911 Walnut Street
23rd Floor
Kansas CIty, MO 64106
816-374-5502

Colorado, Wyoming, Utah, Montana, North Dakota, South Dakota
Procurement Specialist
1405 Curtis Street
22nd Floor
Denver, CO 80202
303-837-5441

Southern California (Zip Codes 90000-93599), Arizona
Procurement Specialist
350 S. Figueroa Street
6th Floor
Los Angeles, CA 90071
213-688-2946

Northern California (Zip Codes 93600-95999), Hawaii, Nevada, Guam
Procurement Specialist
Box 36044
450 Golden Gate Ave.
San Francisco, CA 94102
415-556-9616

Oregon, Idaho, Washington, Alaska
Procurement Specialist
4th and Vine Bldg.
2615 4th Ave.
Seattle, WA 98121
206-442-0390

Federal Procurement Programs

General Services Administration

Although every government agency has its own procurement office, purchases which are exceptionally large or can be planned well in advance are all handled by the General Services Administration. The GSA is in charge of buying a new fleet of cars for the IRS, for example, whereas if an office in the IRS building needed painting, the agency itself would hire the painter. There-fore, if you want to bid on a big contract or a long-term job with the government, the GSA is the agency you'll want to talk to.

The Business Services Center Program of the GSA can help small business owners to find their place in government procurement. This agency acts as an advisory service and consultant to those who are new business owners or who have never done business with the federal government before. Any business is eligible for their advisory services, which range in subject from procurement contracts for products and services to surplus government proper-ty sales contracts, concession contracts, and repair and renova-tion contracts.

One service provided by the GSA is the Office of Small and Disadvantaged Business Utilization. Their programs are aimed specifically at small and women/minority run busi-nesses, and are geared toward insuring that these businesses get their share of government contracts. The Office of Small and Disadvantaged Business Utilization also works with other government agencies to coordinate the use of small, minority, and women run business contracts throughout the government. Additionally, they assist in the legislation and regulation of these type of contracts and in the training of government employees who deal with these businesses. They are there to assure that small businesses do not get lost in the government paperwork shuffle.

Also under the direction of the GSA is the Federal In formation Center. Their sole purpose is to distribute written and verbal information about any government agency or pro-gram, including referral services. Anyone is eligible for assistance from this department.

The General Services Administration has regional offices at the following addresses. Contact the one nearest you for more information:

District of Columbia, Maryland, and Virginia
7th and D Sts. SW Room 1050
Washington, DC 20407
(202) 472-1804

Connecticut, Maine, Massachusetts, New Hampshire, Rhode Island, Vermont
Boston Federal Office Bldg.
10 Causeway St.
Boston, MA 02222
(617) 565-8100

New Jersey, New York, Puerto Rico, U.S. Virgin Islands
26 Federal Plaza
New York, NY 10278
(212) 264-1234

Delaware, Pennsylvania, Maryland, Virginia, West Virginia
9th and Market Sts., Room 5151
Philadelphia, PA 19107
(215) 597-1237

Alabama, Florida, Georgia, Kentucky, Mississippi, North Carolina, South Carolina, Tennessee
Richard B. Russell Federal Bldg. and Courthouse
75 Spring St. SW
Atlanta, GA 30303
(404) 331-5103

Illinois, Indiana, Michigan, Minnesota, Ohio, Wisconsin
230 South Dearborn St.
Chicago, IL 60604
(312) 353-5383

Iowa, Kansas, Missouri, Nebraska
1500 East Bannister Rd.
Kansas City, MO 64131-3088
(816) 926-7203

Arkansas, Louisiana, New Mexico, Oklahoma, Texas
Room 11 A 05
819 Taylor St.
Fort Worth, TX 76102
(817) 334-3284

Colorado, Montana, North Dakota, South Dakota, Utah, Wyoming
Denver Federal Center
PO Box 25006 Rm. 145
Denver, CO 80225-0006
(303) 236-7409

Hawaii, Nevada (except for Clark County), Northern California
525 Market St.
San Francisco, CA 94105
(415) 947-0523

Arizona, Los Angeles, Clark County (Nevada), Southern California
300 North Los Angeles St.
Room 3259
Los Angeles, CA 90012
(213) 894-3210

Alaska, Idaho, Oregon, Washington
Rm 2413
15th and C Sts. SW
Auburn, WA 98001
(206) 931-7956

Offices of Small and Disadvantaged Business Utilization

Every branch of the government with the authority to procure has an Office of Small and Disadvantaged Business Utilization to assure that all aspects of contracting are available to the small businessman. These offices oversee many policies which are intended to make sure that every business has a chance to land a government contract.

One of these policies is the **Small Business Set-Aside Program.** This program requires every government agency to limit competition on certain contracts to "small businesses" (as defined by the SBA). It states that contract awards be given to competitive bids, so business is only set-aside in areas where there is sufficient competition to create realistic prices.

Another policy regulated by the OSDBU is the Labor Surplus Area Set-Aside Program. In areas where unemployment is higher than the national average, such as an area where a large plant or factory has shut down, small businesses can operate under restricted competition if they do most of their business in the economically depressed area. Again, this policy is only enacted when there is enough competition to assure fair and reasonable prices.

When a large corporation is granted a major government contract, the OSDBU steps in to assure that small businesses will not be left out of this procedure. The Subcontracts for Small and Disadvantaged Businesses Policy insures that every company who is granted a prime contract (over $500,000 total value, or $1,000,000 for contraction) must specify the amount of subcontracts which it will grant to small businesses, and exactly how it will go about it. This means that even if you do not acquire a government contract, you may still be able to take advantage of government money.

The OSDBU also urges government agencies to purchase goods from both women owned and veteran owned businesses. They also specify certain goods which, if offered at competitive prices, must be purchased from workshops for the blind and severely handicapped.

Each agency's OSDBU has different policies and procedures for purchasing from small businesses. In order to find out more about specific programs, contact the OSDBU in the department you are interested in doing business with.

Small and Disadvantaged Business Utilization Offices

Executive Office of the President
Director, OSDBU
Washington, DC 20503
(202) 395-3314

Department of Agriculture
Director, OSDBU, Rm. 127 W
Washington, DC 20250
(202) 447-7117

Department of Commerce
Director, OSDBU, Rm. 6411
Washington, DC 20230
(202) 377-3387

Department of Defense
Director, OSDBU, Rm. 2A340
Washington, DC 20307
(202) 694-1151

Defense Logistics Agency
Director, OSDBU, Rm. 4B110
Washington, DC 22304-6100
(703) 274-6471

Department of the Air Force
Director, OSDBU, Rm. 4C255
Washington, DC 20330-5040
(202) 697-4126

Department of the Army
Director, OSDBU, Rm. 2A712
Washington, DC 20301
(202) 695-9800

Department of the Navy
Director, OSDBU, Rm. 604
Washington, DC 20360
(202) 692-7122

Department of Education
Director, OSDBU, Rm. 2141
Washington, DC 20202
(202) 245-9582

Department of Energy
Director, OSDBU, Rm. 1E061

Washington, DC 20585
(202) 252-8201

Department of Health and Human Services
Director, OSDBU, Rm. 531D
Washington, DC 20201
(202) 245-7300

Department of Housing and Urban Development
Director, OSDBU, Rm. 10226
Washington, DC 20240
(202) 755-1485

Department of the Interior
Director, OSDBU, Rm. 2747
Washington, DC 20240
(202) 343-8493

Department of Justice
Director, OSDBU, Rm. 748
HOLC Bldg.
Washington, DC 20530
(202) 724-6271

Department of Labor
Director, OSDBU, Rm. S1004
Washington, DC 20210
(202) 523-9148

Department of State
Director, OSDBU, Rm. 513 (SA-6)
Washington, DC 20520
(202) 235-9579

Department of Transportation
Director, OSDBU, Rm. 10222
Washington, DC 20590
(202) 426-1930

Department of Treasury
Director, OSDBU, Rm. 127 W
Washington, DC 20250
(202) 447-7117

Small Business Administration

Getting a Government Contract

Under the SBA's 8(a) program, the SBA acts as a prime contractor and enters into all types of Federal Government contracts (including but not limited to, supply, services, construction, research and development) with other government departments and agencies and negotiates subcontracts for the performance thereof with small companies in the 8(a) program.

The Purpose of the 8(a) program is to:

1. Foster business ownership by individuals who are socially and economically disadvantaged.

2. Promote the competitive viability of such firms by providing such a viable contract and financial, technical and management assistance as may be necessary.

3. Clarify and expand the program for the procurement of articles, equipment, supplies, service, materials, and construction work from small business concerns owned by socially and economically disadvantaged individuals.

Applicants for participation in the 8(a) program must meet certain criteria. For the specific requirements, ask your local SBA office for FACT SHEET NO. 36.

Remember, like the GSA, the SBA has dozens of programs and plans aimed at helping small businesses get off the ground and become successful. The SBA knows that small business represents a large portion of the American work force; in 1986 alone small businesses were responsible for creating over one million jobs. More than 90% of **all** businesses in the United States are classified as small (by SBA standards). Because of this, the SBA wants to do everything they can to foster new job growth and keep existing jobs open.

As mentioned, the SBA offers programs and policies regarding loans for new and existing businesses, both in the form of debt capital (money that must be returned with interest), and investment capital (money which goes to buy a portion of your business). They do this by either insuring a government loan with their own money, or by lending the money themselves if a bank is unwilling to. They also offer loans to businesses struck by natural disasters, and to businesses in economically disadvantaged areas.

Probably the most highly used of any SBA assistance program, the Service Corps of Retired Executives (SCORE) and the Active Corps of Executives (ACE) provide counseling by businesspeople both retired from and currently in the work force. They focus on management training and counseling, and are an excellent source of experience to draw upon. Currently there are 12,000 such business consultants, all volunteers, who are available for business counseling.

The Business Development Assistance to Small Business Program draws heavily on the SCORE/ACE program. Under this plan, business executives provide advisory services, counseling, technical information, and training to small business management. This is given in the form of seminars, publications, and Small Business Development Centers.

Under the 8(a) Minority Business Development - Procurement Assistance Program, businesspeople who have been deprived of the opportunity to develop and maintain a position in the competitive economy because of a social disadvantage are given a chance to bid on certain government subcontracts. These disadvantaged people include Black, Hispanic, Asian, and Native Americans (but are not limited to these groups.)

The Procurement Assistance to Small Businesses Program provides technical assistance to small businesses during any phase of obtaining and administering government contracts. All existing and potential small businesses are eligible for this assistance.

Department of Commerce

This large and complex government department concerns itself with many different aspects of legislation, from coastal zone management to population census. Its primary function, however, is to promote trade and business both within the United

States and abroad. In order to further this activity, the Department of Commerce makes business loans and gives grants to agencies which advise businesses.

One of the most helpful agencies to small businesses is the Minority Business Development Agency. They sponsor a number of programs aimed at assisting minority owned companies that do business with the government. In 100 Minority Business Development Centers around the country, the MBDA offers technical assistance for all types of businesses in all phases of commerce. This assistance comes from state and local governments, accounting and consulting firms, business consultants, and educational institutions. For more information on how you can benefit from these development centers, contact:

Minority Business Agency, USDC
14th and Constitution Ave. NW - Rm. 6725
Washington, DC 20230
(202) 377-8015

Department of Defense

The Department of Defense is the largest consumer of goods and services in the federal government. Every year the budget allows billions of dollars for the military to spend. Although many of its contracts are completed by huge corporations, the small businessperson still has a chance to work with the DOD either by prime contract work or by sub-contracting to a large company.

While aircraft and missile systems are areas set aside mostly for the big defense manufacturers, small businesses supply up to 90% of the DOD's need for items such as clothing, textiles, food, and construction. These items are procured either by the individual branch of the armed forces, or by the Defense Logistics Agency, which is responsible for making various purchases for the entire DOD. These agencies can be contacted at the following addresses:

ARMY:
Director of Small and Disadvantaged Business Utilization
Office of the Secretary of the Army,

Pentagon
Washington, DC 20310

NAVY:

Director of Small and Disadvantaged Business Utilization
Office of the Secretary of the Navy,
Crystal Plaza No. 6
Washington, DC 20360

AIR FORCE:

Director of Small and Disadvantaged Business Utilization
Office of the Secretary of the Air Force
Pentagon
Washington, DC 20230

DEFENSE LOGISTICS AGENCY:

Staff Directory of Director of Small
and Disadvantaged Business Utilization
Defense Logistics Agency
Cameron Station
Alexandria, VA 22314

GENERAL INFORMATION:

Defense Procurement Information Office
Office of the Deputy Undersecretary of Defense for Research and
Engineering (acquisition policy)
Pentagon
Washington, DC 20301

Under the Section 8(a) Minority Business Development-Procurement Assistance Program, the DOD has a policy whereby certain contracts are given to the Small Business Administration, which in turn sub-contracts them to a number of small business bidders which are kept on file. If you have a service or product which you feel might be helpful to the DOD via a subcontract, you should contact the Small Business Administration.

Nearly every government agency has a procurement office. If you are interested in obtaining a government contract or subcontract, you must try every department and bureau until you find one which will take your bid. The government needs so many services that there is room for nearly every business.

$25,000 For Giving Away Special Disks

This is the Easiest Money in the World

Can you imagine making at least $20,000 this week? I absolutely guarantee you can with this amazing system I have discovered. All you have to do is give away "special disks" that you can get absolutely free with my program. Give away a batch of my "special disks," and you can earn a minimum of $20,000. All you do is give away "special disks" to be making millions like other people have.

Twenty thousand dollars for giving away "special disks" that you can get free with my program. I absolutely guarantee that you have never seen anything like this program in your life. It is a brainstorm that can make you rich beyond your wildest dreams. Why shouldn't it? It has made hundreds of people very rich. It is in such demand by millions of people all over the world that millionaires are being created overnight just because they are giving away special disks.

These disks are not a letter or any type of sales article. I guarantee it is an item that can be kept in people's homes and under no circumstances will it ever be thrown away. Each disk is extremely valuable. Many people need these disks very badly and can't do without them, and must have them right away. These disks are considered so valuable that people have paid up to $3,000 a disk. This is no exageration or fluffery but the absolute truth. Thousands have been paid for a single disk, and not by just a few people but thousands of people have paid up to $3,000 a disk. Just knowing this, imagine how people feel when they find out you are giving away these valuable disks. You will be trampled over in their mad rush to get these valuable disks from you. The more you give away the more you make. Don't worry, you won't have even the slightest problem giving away these disks, your only problem will be not having enough of these valuable wonders. Giving away this "unique package" is easy. People need it and want it badly. I know this because thousands of people who have this item have told me so.

They can make you more cash than you have ever seen in your life for doing practically nothing. It is a "special disk" system that you will find mind boggling. You will fall on the floor when you see how badly these special disks are needed and how very few people are providing them. I guarantee this system 100%; this method could make you hundreds of thousands with very little effort in a short time. Follow my instructions on giving away "special disks" that you can get free. You can make a minimum of $20,000 this week when you start giving away "special disks."

People using my method have an income in the hundreds of thousands of dollars. They are giving away "special disks" and are making hundreds of thousands of dollars. Not thousands, but hundreds of thousands because it is so new, so fresh and so badly needed in this country. I am giving you a ground floor opportunity to sit back in a chair and watch thousands of hundred dollar bills roll into your fingers. It is a method of making money with no catches that can give you financial glory beyond your wildest dreams. Forty thousand dollars could be yours.

Here is absolute Proof

- A 40 year-old man from Fort Worth, Texas, is giving away thousands of "special disks" every day. Immediately after starting his program he was earning $37,000 a month. In less than a year he was earning $105,000 a month.
- A very successful, 63 year-old doctor from Encinitas, California, got rid of his high-profit, four-doctor medical center, just so he could use the "special disk" give-away program. He opened a brand new company in Encinitas, California. They are earning $50,000 a month giving away these "special disks" after just opening a short time.
- A man from Chicago, Illinois has been giving away "free disks" for the past few years. They started their "special disk" give-away program for a $50 investment. After the first year they are earning over a hundred thousand dollars a month. An entrepreneur from Oklahoma City, Oklahoma was unsuccessful with almost every business he tried, then he started the disk give-away program. He was able to make a whopping $1.3 million a year, with no training, or large investment or skills.
- An elderly man from Van Nuys, California with no education or skills started giving away "special disks" in December. After a few weeks he quit his job and hired his family and five other employees. He also bought a brand new car, a new home and began earning $42,000 a month. He earned 10 times what he was earning just previously.

I am very eager to tell you about this remarkable method that is like no other money-making plan you have ever seen in your life. It will make the American Dream become a reality for you. Hundreds of thousands of dollars can be yours when you give away the "special disks" that I supply you absolutely free. That is all you have to do to enjoy an easy, relaxing, laid back, wealthy lifestyle.

$2,500 Guarantee

Order my book on giving away "special disks" and spend a few hours reading the book. If you can prove to me that the methods in the book couldn't make anyone hundreds of thousands of dollars like they have made other people, I will send you a check for the full amount of $2,500 direct to your door. I am only doing this because I

stand behind this "special disk" give-away system. You will be filled with amazement when you see how badly this unique package is needed and how nobody is providing it at all. I absolutely guarantee that this plan can make you at least $20,000 with very little effort. It is time that you enjoy the great luxuries my "unique package" system can get you.

My Guarantee

Order my "special disk" program. Read the first three chapters. Go over the free disks I send you. (These free disks are sold by other companies for $20 a disk, but they are yours free). You are going to love it. It is easy to use, yet it will flood you with mounds of cash.

Disks are limited. I can't guarantee any free disks or my program after 30 days. You must send off for my program right now to be assured delivery.

You can make more cash than you have ever seen in your life for giving away "special disks." I know you will find this "special disk" give-away system the greatest discovery of your life. Your eyes will be filled with amazement when you see how badly this unique package is needed and how nobody is providing it at all. I absolutely guarantee that this plan can make you a lot of money with very little effort. If you could use $20,000 a week you need my "special disk" system. It is time that you enjoy the great luxuries my "special disk" system can get you. Don't delay, rush my mind-boggeling "special disk" program to your door. Do this and you can be set for life. Get your program today!!!

FREE CASH GRANT INSIDER SOURCES

Can you imagine that within a few minutes of calling me, you will know where the free money is located? The secret treasure map that shows you how to get thousands upon thousands of free cash grants could be yours. The same information that is sold for up to a few hundred dollars can be yours when you call me! LEARN CONFIDENTIAL, SPECIAL ADDRESSES, PHONE NUMBERS, LOOPHOLES AND TECHNIQUES THAT COULD GET YOU ALL THE FREE MONEY GRANTS YOU NEED. If you call this very second, you will be told in just a few minutes from now all of these vital techniques and loopholes, as well as everything you need to know to get a free cash grant. That's free money that you never ever have to pay back. It is your permanent cash gift. I won't try to sell you a bunch of books and courses that don't even tell you what you need to know. No sales B.S. from me. I'm not going to do this to you. NO WAY! I will just give you the straight facts. It's going to take from a few weeks to a few months for their stuff to reach you. That's crazy. Heck, if you have to wait a few months, you won't need the free money any more. Any fool knows that if you need a free grant, you want the money right now. All you get from me is immediate, important sources of free money that you can use right away. I believe in instant gratification. Call me and learn the secrets of getting free cash grants within the next few minutes.

Call me right now, and I will spill my guts out, and tell you my confidential sources and simple techniques on how you can get free grants. A few minutes from now your ears will be privileged to hear extremely vital information. Information that could overflow your bank account with free mega-cash gifts. The cash is yours for the asking with no obligation to ever pay it back. Forget about getting a loan to solve your money problems, because I will tell you over the phone how and where to get free cash grants. This free windfall money has nothing to do with your credit or financial history. In fact, in some cases, having bad credit will help you get these free grants. So what are you waiting for? Information that is only known by the privileged few, can be yours.

THEY MUST GIVE IT AWAY

I'm a straight shooter and will only tell you the honest truth. The free grant information you will hear when you call is extremely valuable. I won't give you sources that will hang up on you or return your letters, but you will get phone numbers and addresses of places that must give their grant money away (they must by law) to people like you. If they don't give their money away, they lose their tax status, and all the grant administrators will lose their jobs. They would never let this happen. These institutions absolutely must give their money away. They have a quota to fill. Meet their simple requirements and you will be showered with cold cash. I guarantee you will be utterly astounded by how many free money grants are available and how easy they are to get. It's mind boggling; you will be in for the shock of your life. Be prepared to fall on your face when you see how little you have to do to qualify for their free grant money. (Being a minority, being over 65, having certain last names, being broke, being handicapped, wanting to make home repairs, wanting to start certain businesses, the list goes on and on.)

THEY GOT FREE GRANTS

- Two men who ran a dining room in Arizona got a $160,000 grant so that they could hire nine more employees.
- A group in Vermont received a $45,000 grant so that they could start a facility to produce wood burning stoves.
- Barbara Kopple received $27,980 in free money to create a film about coal miners.
- Deborah H. from Austin, Texas got $7,500 worth of grants to set up a dance production.
- Ira Wohl received a grant of $25,000 to produce a film called "Best Boys."
- An inventor in New Orleans, Harry E. W., received a $72,000 grant to aid his company that produced water heaters. This grant allowed Harry to expand his current operations.
- Al D., from Gloucester, Massachusetts received grants totaling $300,000 to create a community center for teenagers.

HERE'S MY NUMBER

Calling me isn't free. There is a small charge. **Calling my number 900-468-4726,** costs $2 the first minute and 45 cents each additional minute. But believe me this charge is nothing compared to all the free money you will get. If you think that a few dollars is too much to pay to get vital phone numbers and addresses, I urge you not to call under any circumstances. In fact, you should tear up this page into tiny pieces, just in case you have the urge to get a free cash grant. Only a fool would waste a few dollars to get a $100,000 grant that never has to be payed back, ever; especially because these grants have made many common people (some in debt) very rich. These are all bad reasons to call. If that is your logic, there is nothing I can do for you, calling is a waste of time. You know what they say, those who think small, become small.

Those who think big, become big. How do you think? What do you want to be?

If you call, you will hear in the next few minutes the easiest-to-qualify for and the rarest confidential sources of free grant money. **Look at your watch, make the call to me and you will see for yourself how quickly vital, secret phone numbers and addresses will be known to you.** Have a pen and paper handy, you will need them badly. Make sure your pen doesn't run out of ink. If it runs out of ink in the middle of my important message, you may suffer from a nervous breakdown. I don't want that to happen, so make sure you place two pens by the phone while you listen to my miracle message.

ONE CONDITION

I only want you to call me under one condition. **When you get your free grant I want you to remember who helped you get it. I will give you extremely vital information. I want to see you succeed.** After all, you will learn incredible secrets for spare change. After you get the free grant money, remember me. Allow me to help you manage and spend your newly found free grant money wisely. I can help you mushroom your newly found grant money into your own huge financial empire. When you make your first million dollars, we might even work together on a multi-million dollar operation. It's a "win," "win" situation. I help you now and you help me later. This way we will all prosper together. I will teach you how to get that free grant money that could change your life around. You are so close to making it big; just a phone call away. Let's get your life going on the right track. Let's do it now.

Call me and in an instant you will know how and where to get free money grants. I will not bore you with this history of grants or other useless information, but, right off the bat, I will give you phone numbers and addresses of confidential places that could give you car loads of free grant money. Your dreams could be fulfilled within minutes of listening to my vital information. My message could utterly change your life forever. Don't call because I tell you to, call because this number will change your life forever. It will change it so much, you will never be the same. **My vital free grant information that you will learn, will show you how to put free money in your hands. I will show you how to load your bank account with grant money that you will never have to pay back. It is yours forever no matter what.** Don't hesitate, call right now. If you need the money, you absolutely must call.

Government grants are available for certain types of businesses, education, real estate and other investment projects, but not for every imaginable purpose. Special assistance programs and low interest loans are available, however, for almost any type of business, real estate, education or other investment project.

Let Two Minutes Change Your Life

I will tell you in two minutes about special confidential addresses that could earn you thousands of dollars. That's right, call me and I will dictate special addresses that could earn you more money than you can use. I am not going to sell you a book; besides, very few books contain this valuable, almost-impossible-to-obtain information. **You will be given all the particulars for an instant plan that could make you $10,000 this week.** Secret information that is only known by a select few could be yours, and all you have to do is write down what I tell you. Not only will you get confidential addresses, but I will also tell you who to contact and what to put in your letter. When you call, have a pencil and paper ready because that is all you will need to make big money. If you can write, you have the skills needed to make money with me.

INSTANT CASH

Call me and write down the addresses and the simple insider instructions that I will give you. Do this and you will be on your way to the big time. You will be in the money almost instantly. What could be easier? These priceless two minutes could solve all of your money problems forever. All of your money troubles could be non-existent. Just think about how easy it will be to make money, all of this for one simple two-minute phone call. What's more, there are no costly books or courses to buy. Why would anyone want to buy expensive books and courses when I can give you the confidential addresses that you'll need? You will get addresses of places that will give you needed cash just for writing them a letter. After all, most opportunity books have only one paragraph of value, the rest of the book is just a pile of B.S. Doesn't that bother you? It drives me crazy. You read and read and read and read, but you have learned nothing. Then all of a sudden, one page tells you everything you want to know. They could have put that one system on one page so why write the book? When you call, I will give you the juicy meat, none of that fluffy filler. You can be sure of that. I supply you with the vital information you need to become independently wealthy. All of this for the most important two minutes of your life. Two hundred and sixty seconds that could stuff your bank account with hundreds of thousands of dollars. This is an insider system that will earn you huge amounts of money for doing practically nothing. If you can write the confidential information I will dictate to you, you have the skills needed to make big money with me.

HERE'S WHAT I NEED FROM YOU

All this vital money-making information is yours just for listening to me. I will dictate the priceless information while you write it down. You should have at least one 8 1/2" × 11" sheet in front of you when you call. Don't use a small message pad, because I will give you insider tips that are worth thousands. I know when I start disclosing my vital tips, you will be in a fit of urgency, madly writing them all down. Believe me, it's going to hurt if you don't have enough paper to write it all down. One 34-year-old man from Ohio ran out of paper and had to write all over his hands and feet. He called me and told me he bet people would pay him hundreds of dollars to take his clothes off. Could you see yourself tattooed with hundreds of thousands of dollars of vital information? You would be a walking bank. Don't forget to have more than one pen or pencil in front of you also. If your pen breaks, you may experience the greatest disaster of your life. This will probably be the only time your pen will be worth its weight in gold.

ULTIMATE PROOF

So far what I have told you sounds utterly amazing. It all is absolutely true, though. If you made the phone call you would know this. Let me share with you how some skeptical people felt about this amazing information. **"I got $10,000 in free money for two different projects that were used on the Section 8 Program." Clare N., St. Louis, MO. Harry E., from New Orleans received $72,000 absolutely free for his company that produces water heaters. Deborah M., from Hollywood, California received 1.75 million dollars in cash and benefits to build a fitness center in California. Rose and Jim T., from Minneapolis, received $50,000 to work on a pizza restaurant. Due to their assistance from a confidential source they went from selling 25 pizzas a day to 200,000. Because of the assistance they received they are now multi-millionaires. You could have this kind of success and you could be earning millions of dollars. The choice is yours. You are one phone call away from millions of dollars.**

ONE THREE MINUTE CALL

You can now call one phone number that will give you valuable information. You will not be listening to someone trying to sell you something. All you will get is confidential addresses that supply people with instant cash within a week. You will get some vital tips that have never been disclosed before. All you need is a pen and a piece of paper and you could get free money as early as this week. **The 24-hour phone number to call is: 1-900-468-2255. In California—1-900-468-6663.** There is a charge for this phone call: $2 for the first minute and 45¢ for each additional minute. If this charge is going to hurt you, don't call. There are people who won't call to get these valuable addresses because they have to pay a few dollars. These people think small and are always in debt and have no chance of ever getting rich. (Do you know anyone who wouldn't invest a few dollars to make thousands of dollars easily? After all, I am taking all the risk with my special guarantee.) I urge these small people to burn this ad, so that they may not accidentally call this number at a later date. If these small people were to call this number, thousands of dollars in free money could be theirs. Once they get this free money, they wouldn't know what to do with it. It is better that this easy-to-obtain free money is collected by the positive, go-getters who know a good thing when they see it. The only thing small people will accomplish is to make my phone number busy, and that will prevent future millionaires from getting my valuable information. I am so sure that the information I will reveal to you will knock your socks off, that I will offer you an absolutely unheard-of guarantee. A guarantee that I know you will not be able to resist. Let me tell you more about it.

TEN TIMES YOUR MONEY

I will put my money where my mouth is. If you can prove to me that some of the information I give you has not earned others thousands of dollars, send me your phone bill and I will send you a certified check for ten times the amount you spent to call me. Only a fool would not call with a guarantee like this. It lets you call me with no risk. No matter what you do, you should make a lot of money. The key lies in your phone. Call me and you will win. You would be crazy not to call. No matter what happens you will end up a winner. If you want to be a winner, you must call. But I'm not stupid, I wouldn't offer this guarantee if I didn't have valuable information to offer you. If you want to be a loser, don't call. The choice is yours. To 99% of people the decision is obvious. It really depends on where you want to be in the future. Would you like to live day by day just making sure you don't get evicted from your home, or would you like to be sitting in your Mercedes convertible in front of your beautiful mansion by the ocean? Call today and change your life.

New Books & Moneymaking Opportunities

Work At Home Riches

by John Collins

Tired of working for someone else? Then it's time to create your own business at home and make MONEY! This sourcebook is a complete guide for home-based work, giving you insider secrets such as which businesses to get into and suggestions on how to set up your business. Valuable information includes: • How to market your product or service • Over 300 work-at-home sources • Insurance for the home business • Tax and zoning codes • How to run a successful mail-order business • Over 60 drop-shippers, plus prices and product description AND MUCH, MUCH MORE! If you plan a home business, then this book is a "must have!"
#0888; $15

$100,000 Refunds From The U.S.

Could you use a share of the hundreds of millions of dollars of government refunds waiting for you? This is a cash windfall which has added $288,000,000 every year to the pot. All you have to do to get this cash windfall is to send off one letter to the address given in this book. One letter and you could be thousands richer! A special office in the federal gov't housing department is authorizing these refunds. Not only could you be eligible for these gov't refunds, but if you are not, the book shows you how to get 30% finder's fee to deliver this money to someone who is eligible for a refund. That's hundreds of millions of dollars waiting to go back to the American people. Countless numbers of Americans are due this money. There are millions in finder's fees you could cash in on. Get this book today.　　　#5422; $15.00

Take My Free Unique Packages

Could you use $50,000 for distributing unique packages that are supplied with this program? You make money for distributing unique packages that are supplied free with the program. Not only that, but the program shows you how you can get unique packages absolutely free! You get them free and you can make millions distributing them. One man from Alabama made over a million dollars last year distributing unique packages. One man from Toronto made $10,000 his first week out. Another man from La Mesa bought a $200,000 home only months after using the unique package system of making money. The unique packages come free with the program, all you have to do is distribute them and you are on your way to making millions like many others. The unique package system could make you rich.　　　#1335; $12

The Amazing Method Of Reading People

by Tom Foster

Imagine walking into a crowd and being an instant hit just because you know how to "read" women. Read beautiful women instantly with this amazing method. It is easy and effective. If you can tell the difference between a smile and a frown you will be able to use this method. Many government agencies use this sure-fire method of seeing through women.
#0533; $10

$25 Billion Treasure

by David Bendah

Right now the states are holding billions of dollars of unclaimed money. You could make thousands of dollars by just returning this money to the rightful owners. People have made up to $2,000 an hour returning money to lost owners. One man in Texas made over $300,000 from finder's fees on unclaimed money. Studies show that one in ten Americans have unclaimed money coming to them. You could have money owed to you. This book is the greatest manual ever written on getting unclaimed money. It is 300 pages filled with vital information to profit from the government riches of unclaimed money.
#3633; $25

Building Your Million Dollar Empire

Everyone knows that the key to making large amounts of money lies in Real Estate. You can practically buy real estate for nothing down and in some cases you can get money back for buying some real estate. This book will show you how to get into Real Estate without cash. Real Estate is a solid investment...an investment that will increase for years to come...an investment that can make you a millionaire. You must own a piece of America if you truly want to become a millionaire.
#5133; $10

Grey Market Riches

by Dan Webster

Beautiful Porches as well as Mercedes could be parked in front of your house and could be earning you as much as $20,000 each. Did you ever dream that driving luxury cars could make you so much money? This book will show you how to buy almost any luxury car overseas at a fraction of what it costs in this country. Buy cars overseas without leaving your home. All you have to do is make a simple call to Europe and $20,000 is yours. It is easy as that.
#1733; $19.95

Instant Debt Relief And Instant Cash

This five-section, three-book series is a must for anyone who needs money or needs to get out of debt. Section One will give you inside information on how to get loans from secretive sources, including foreign and overseas banks. Section Two will show you how to get major credit cards even if you have bad credit or have been bankrupt. Mastercard, Visa, Discover, Diners Club and American Express cards are waiting for you! Section Three will show you how to get out of debt no matter how bad your credit situation is. Bankrupt or divorce is this section's specialty. Section Four will show you how to start getting a AAA-1 credit rating in a matter of days. Use this credit rating to buy a new business, or just an apartment building, with positive cash flow. Section Five will show you how to get some of the billions of dollars of free money that foundations give away every year. It is a complete debt relief and instant cash program that could get you up to $1,000,000 of cash, which you could put to good use. #9933; $29.95

Cashvision

by Jeff Peters
Imagine watching T.V. while you are making money. Watching your favorite shows could pay off for you with this book, which shows you how to make money with your favorite T.V. shows. A man from California made a whooping $9,000,000 in one year from T.V. shows. Another man from Arizona made over $4,000,000 with the same progam that is outlined in this book. This book is creating a sensation. Everyone can now cash in on their T.V. set. Watching T.V. can now be profitable. Why watch T.V. for nothing, when you can use cashvision to make you rich? Use this exciting book to make money with your T.V.
#2744; $12.95

$4,000 A Day Giving Away Special Books

by Pete Branin
Here is an exciting program that could earn you up to $4,000 a day giving away special books. These special books are a promotional program needed by small businesses. Small businesses have reported increases as much as 500% because of these special books. A man in Florida is making $2,000,000 a year using this special book give-away method. This person has been doing this for five years and is increasing the amount of money he makes every year. This book is based on a $2,000 course, so you know you will get a lot for your money. Cash-in on special books.
#1336; $12

Billion Dollar Modeling Industry

by Jeff Peters
Imagine making thousands of dollars while meeting and working with beautiful women. Women that will beg you to use them in your next shoot. A business where you control the most gorgeous and exotic women in the world. Earn thousands of dollars an hour and you don't even have to do a thing. This book is your ticket to the glamour business of the 80's. It is hot and ready for individuals like yourself to enter. Everything you need to know to make big money in the modeling business is explained to you.
#1033; $12.95

Making $500,000 A Year In Mail-Order

by David Bendah
If you ever dreamed of having your mailbox crammed with thousands of envelopes each containing a check in your name, then this book can make those dreams a reality. Filled with helpful information and secrets of the mail-order trade, this book shows the secret formulas that you can use to get rich.
(6 × 9, 200 pp.) #1233; $15

Winning At The Horse Races

by Paul Lawrence
Can you imagine knowing exactly which horse will finish first before the race starts? This system could put millions of dollars in your pocket every year. It is a 27-part, scientific system that is guarateed to give you results. If you have a calculator and five minutes, you're in business. You could be picking winning horses with this method. Become the racetrack guru with this amazing method.
#1933; $19.95

The Self Publisher's Opportunity Kit

This book is all you need to make money in mail order. It includes eight books that you can sell by mail. They come with reprint rights, which allows you to reprint and sell as many copies as you wish. One man selling these books is making $14.50 profit on every $15 sale. That is a whopping 3000% profit margin.
#1633; $30

Cashing In On Government Money

by Bill Kerth
Could you use at least $30,000 that is owed to you by Uncle Sam and is available just for the asking? Imagine receiving check after check just for filling out the proper forms. There are many government programs for 1989 that you have probably never heard of, that could make you very rich. You could buy a new home for just $1. Uncle Sam foots the rest of the bill. How about getting Uncle Sam to buy you a McDonald's franchise? One man from Houston, Texas got Uncle Sam to buy him two McDonald's resturants. If you can use these 1989 benefits owed to you, you need this book.
#5033; $12.95

Thousands With Your Camera

by Jeff Peters
How would you like to get paid thousands of dollars just for taking simple pictures? You don't even have to be a skilled photographer to use this revolutionary method of making thousands with your camera. This method is so revolutionary that most photographers have never even heard about this method of making money with a camera. Follow the simple instructions—just aim your camera, take the picture and the money is yours—it is as simple as that.
#2733; $12.95

Poor Man's Way To Riches, Volume 1

by David Buckley

David Buckley has left a legacy that will enable you to inherit riches. "Widely regarded as the publisher and author of the best self-help books in the world, he has helped thousands of people rid themselves of former debts and get a fresh start on a successful new life." The 4-volume set of books entitled the *Poor Man's Way to Riches* can offer you a fresh start toward a financially secure future. The first volume of this valuable series contains help on topics that will help you clear off old debts and start on the new financial future. It will tell you how to have: AAA-1 Credit Everywhere • Borrow Money Fast • Raise Tremendous Amounts of Capital • Make a Million Dollars in Real Estate • Take Over Going Businesses With Zero Cash • Earn $5,000 Monthly by Mail • One-Man Businesses That Can Make You Rich • How to Avoid Taxes Legally, and more!
#3033; $10

Volume 2

Volume 2 tells you how to: Earn $30,000 Monthly From Oil Income • Get a Cash Loan From Your State • Obtain Foundation Grants and Loans • Build a $20,000 Coin Collection From Pennies • Enter a Lottery You Can't Lose • Get 24% on Your Savings • Seven Offshore Big Money Lenders • Cash in on Arab Money • Free Patents From NASA.
#3133; $10

Volume 3

Volume 3 tells you how to: Turn $1,000 Into $250,000 • $100,000 in 90 Days With Discount Books • Invest in Machine Guns (149% a Year Profits) • Buy a Home For $75,000 and Sell It For $260,000 • Earn Up to $400 an Hour From Woodcarvings • Become a New Car Broker • $500,000 Yearly From Cordwood Sales • Sell $2,000 Memberships in Survival Retreats • Make $50,000 a Year With a Newsletter Digest • Roll in Profits With Electric Vehicles • Sell Solar Energy Systems • Make $300,000 Yearly With Strategic Metals.
#3233; $10

Volume 4

Volume 4 tells you how to: Make $20,000 a Month With Debt Consolidation • $1,200 a Week With ID Cards • A Business Making $60,000 a Day • Sell Platinum from Auto Catalytic Converters • Grow Big Bucks From Jojoba Farming • Make $1,950 Daily From Photography • Invest in Pennies and Confederate Money • Make Huge Commissions as a Patent Broker • $150,000 Yearly as a manufacturers Representative • $25,000 Part-time from Senior Service • How to Make $4,600 in Five Days.
#3333; $10

Home Business Opportunities

by Russ von Hoelscher

Small business/home business authority Russ von Hoelscher offers you scores of new, dynamic, unusual and proven ways to make lots of money in the comfort of your own home. In addition to almost 100 home business money-making plans (most of which can be started with little or no investment) the author offers in-depth sections on making money in mail order and how to prosper as an information-age "how to" author and/or publisher. Take advantage of this volume to make money at home. Order it today, so you may stay home and still be a money-making success.
#0877; $15

Cashing In On Government Surplus

by Edward Kelly

NOW is the time to start saving on cars, boats, homes and more! This manual tells you which government sales offer the items YOU want and how to get on their mailing lists. How would you like new cameras, fine wines, liquors and much more, all at fantastic savings? Who wouldn't! Do you want a new car? Exciting, nearly-new cars, such as Porsches and Mercedes, are available at pennies-on-the-dollar! All of these expensive items are waiting for you at the special auctions discussed in this manual. Never been to an auction before? The author helps the novice auction-bidder by giving practical auction-bidding tips. Also, find out which auctions sell homes at fantastic, low prices! Save like never before on repossessed luxury items! Send for this manual today!
#0938; $14.95

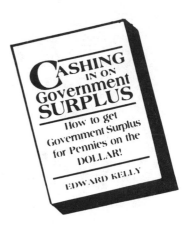

Getting $100,000 of Free Advertising

by George F. Stone

What's better than low-cost advertising? FREE advertising! With this book, find out about free ads and little known publications which are yours for the asking. Learn about how to get free, full TV coverage for your product and how to make millions of dollars with this information! Other topics covered include: * Getting radio to make money for you, without paying for air time * Saving 17% on every ad you place * Getting thousands of orders for your products just by sending out simple letters * Getting other people to advertise your products by direct mail, absolutely free AND MUCH, MUCH MORE! If saving money on your advertising is important to you, then this book is an absolute MUST!
#4053; $15

Getting the Government to Pay for Your New Business

by George F. Strong

So you need $50,000 to $100,000 to start a new business? Ok! The government, your friend-in-need, can also be you ace-in-the-hole. Uncle Sam is waiting for you to ask him to be your partner! This book will tell you: what motivates the government, so you know what they're looking for; what government assistance is available and how you can be "partners" with Uncle Sam. You'll find out which departments and publications are waiting to help YOU! Included are lists of offices which exist to assist you and a sample loan application proposal. Get the help you deserve today!
#4055; $15

Making TV and Radio Advertising Pay Off

by George F. Strong

Would you like to know how to get national coverage of your product for only $15 a minute? What products sell like crazy on cable TV? What airing times will increase your sales 13 times? These answers and much more are in George F. Strong's book on TV and radio advertising. Also covered is: * How to make millions a month selling by TV * A method of getting free air time for your product * What type of program is a hot money-maker * Six subliminal ways to get people to order your product * Which stations will save you thousands AND MUCH, MUCH MORE! Order today to make radio and TV pay off for you!
#4052; $15

Take Your Junk Mail to the Bank

by Larry Miller
Don't laugh at this idea, you CAN take your junk mail and "turn it into cash." The junk mail you receive in your home could be worth thousands of dollars! This manual tells you how you could be making up to $1,500 or more, simply by filling out a form and putting it into the mail. If you get 10 pieces of junk mail a week, you could get back $350 a week. So, that means that 20 to 100 pieces might bring $700 to $3,500 next week! Send for this manual today to learn how to "turn your junk mail into cash."
#0637; $12

How to Make a Fortune from Direct Mail

by George F. Strong
If you've always wanted to start your own business and get paid everyday, then you'll never have a better chance than by starting your own mail-order business. This book gives you a direct mail overview and specific information on planning your campaign and creating a direct mail package. Learn about the importance of mailing lists in this "age of information," including generating your own lists and making big bucks from them! Since you'll never see your customers in the direct mail business, it's important that you have your mailing piece, business forms, cards, etc. printed by quality printers. This book tells you about printing, what to look for and how to avoid trouble. After your direct mail piece is printed, how do you test its effectiveness? Chapter Six tells you several effective testing methods and Chapter Seven gives you insider's secrets on fulfilling customers orders to make you the most money. Get started today on this exciting career of the 90's!
#4050; $15

Making Money From Display and Classified Ads

by George F. Strong
Learn the insider secrets of display and classified advertising for your direct mail business in this comprehensive book. Would you like to know how to word your ad so that the reader has no choice but to buy your product? Which part of the newspaper will get you 10 times the ad cost in results? This book tells you these facts and much more! Some of the information includes: * What you place in the headline of your ad to triple ad sales * What type of picture to place in your ad to double response rate * What guarantee to use that assures you a sale almost every time * What to place in the coupon to make sure twice as many people send you money right away * What words in a classified ad will get you thousands of dollars for practically nothing * How to cut your ad cost by as much as 50% in many publications. AND MUCH, MUCH MORE!
#4051; $15

You Can Make Millions In the Import/Export Market

by Samuel P. Wood
Join the world market with these two books! In the first book, you receive information on setting up your business, finding a name, getting the right product to sell and finding and contacting suppliers. You get insider information on mail-order sales and how and when to advertise. Learn the exciting world of drop-ship selling and how to make more sales with less time and effort. The second book includes two sections: "The Government and You" and "Finding Capital." You'll learn about transportation, orders and payments and getting the maximum profit for your import. Extensive lists of capital sources, foreign embassies, U.S. Customs offices and exporters/manufacturers complete this extensive book. A complete package of money-making information!
#3729; $29.95

Stay Home and Make Money

by Russ von Hoelscher
Full-time or spare-time, you can start making big profits in the safety and comfort of your own home. This exciting book presents you with scores of new, proven, profitable ways to have your cake and eat it too. This is really four books in one: 1) How to get started right and avoid the pitfalls 2) Home business opportunities that are hot right now; money-making plans 3) Writing/publishing services that people want and will pay you handsomely for (writing experience unneccessary) 4) Special, big profit opportunities in direct marketing and mail order AND MUCH, MUCH MORE! Includes the "Ten Commandments" of home businesses and how to avoid the five major mistakes that threaten every home business.
#2656; $15

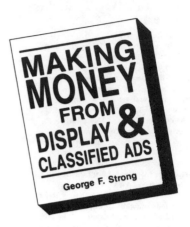

$12,000 Guaranteed in Just 3 Minutes

by Sam Pitts
Want to receive cash by answering your phone? The author shows you how! Sam says this method of making money with his phone earned him from $400 to $29,000 for each three minute phone call. With this method, he earned $568,554.16 in four months! Many people have tried his program with great success. One man from New York, John Liberto, says "Your money-making secret is ringing my phone off the hook with calls amounting into thousands of dollars." If you would like to have YOUR phone earn you money, order this book.
#0636; $12.95

Making Millions From Free Products

by George F. Strong
There's no better way to keep profits high than to keep overhead low, and getting your products free, or next to nothing, is the best way of all! In this book, you learn insider secrets about where to get these amazing bargains. Bonus information includes importing products and protecting your products once you have them. You, too, can be among the few who truly understand the value of making millions from free products.
#3730; $15

Buy Real Estate With Nothing Down

by Phillip Wellington

Here's how you can have a real estate empire using no money of your own! Get your feet wet in the real estate market, without any cash. This book tells it all. You'll find out how, with little or no money down, you can buy real estate without using any of your own money! Here, you'll get insider information on all the traditional ways to finance PLUS all the exciting, new ways to raise money. Learn how to negotiate a deal with the property seller, use equity sharing and leverage. Also, find out how to actually get the seller to HELP YOU with the financing! Phillip Wellington's system tells you how. Order today to get started buying real estate with nothing down.
#3858; $15

Getting Real Estate Next to Nothing with Bankruptcies and Auctions

by Phillip Wellington

Learn how to take advantage of bankruptcy sales, Veterans Administration repossessed property sales and much more! This dynamic book lists all of the many government auctions and summarizes each for YOU. How much do you know about U.S. Customs Service auctions, local police auctions, U.S. Post Office auctions, trustee sales, sheriff's sales and tax sales? The author has brought over 14 houses and numerous cars at such auctions. This book shows how YOU can save at these auctions. Order today start saving!
#3860; $15

Get Rich With Foreclosures

by Phillip Wellington

Once you see the insider secrets for making millions in the real estate business, you'll know why there is no better way to get rich faster than with real estate! How to get distressed property at a fraction of its worth is explained step-by-step in this book. The author leads you by the hand through the foreclosure process to show you what to do when you find such property and how you, too, can get these amazing savings! As a bonus, the author covers the renovation process on fixer-upper property, making your investment grow by leaps and bounds! This is a "must buy" for the serious real estate investor.
#3861; $15

Become a Real Estate Millionaire

by Phillip Wellington

Here is the big picture of what's possible for YOU in the world of real estate. In this book, the author gets you started with the insider terms that will open doors for you. You get special knowledge of the inner workings of the property-game, including: tax advantages, capitalization and cash-flow. You learn how to get rich using other people's money. Buy valuable, commercial property for "no down." How to you find the best investment properties, such as rental units? This book gives YOU all the insiders' tips on finding, financing, renovating and maintaining rentals...and keeping them rented! Want to grow even larger? Use leap-frogging to increase your financial clout. Make your investment grow right before your eyes with the knowledge gained from this book!
#3862; $15

Capital Raising Digest

by Joseph Wright

So you need mega-bucks? This book will help you find your way through the financing jungle with solid information on raising money both for yourself and for others. This is designed for two types of people: those who want to borrow money for their own use and those who want to establish their own financial brokerage business. You'll learn how to set-up your brokerage business, the ABC's of borrowing, how to read and use financial reports and how to get mega-bucks from lenders outside the country! This is the book you need!
#9934; $15

Get Out Of Debt Forever

by Joseph Wright

You can get out of debt forever and receive AAA-1 credit! This exciting book tells you how to erase bad debt and get an SBA loan. You'll learn about personal and debt loan companies, venture capital and minority business development agencies. Do you know what an SBIC is? I tell you how SBIC can help you. Includes information on the General Services Administration regional offices and lists other important agencies. This book is a "must have" if you want out of debt.
#9935; $15

The Secrets of Getting Free Money

by Joseph Wright

Do you see others like yourself, but who seem to have a lot more money? Learn the secrets of raising large amounts of money in this outstanding book. I tell you how to get free money from many sources, including grants from a foundation that you never have to pay back! Learn all the financial secrets that others know. It helps them to get ahead. Isn't it time YOU got ahead instead of always running to catch up? This book can lead you to greater financial freedom and riches. It's the book you need.
#3740; $15

How to Get Any Credit Card You Want, Even If You Have Bad Credit

by Joseph Wright

Time to get out of the "credit hole" and create a new life for yourself. This book tells you what your credit reputation is, how it is determined and how knowing all this information will aid in controlling your credit destiny. You find out how to put your feet on the road to good credit. Included is a complete, systemized approach to getting that good credit. Also contains a comprehensive list of low-interest credit cards available nationwide. Take that first step to creating a new life of credit for YOU!
#9937; $15

Let the U.S. Government Make Your Fortune in Real Estate

by Phillip Wellington

Why should you use your hard-earned money to buy real estate when the government has millions of dollars available in FHA/HUD loans? In this book you'll learn about the dept. of Housing and Urban Development (HUD) programs and the Farmer's Home Administration (FmHA) programs. I tell you all the insider's tricks for investing in FHA foreclosed property, medical care facilities, mobile homes, mobile home parks and MORE!
#3859; $15

How To Get Anything You Want Absolutely Free Or Next To Nothing

by Phil Williams

Learn how to find those exclusive bargains and get products for free in this new book. Learn how to get bargains at closeouts, get government surplus, get goods for 10 cents on the dollar and many other bargains that seem too good to be true. #4733; $10

Make A Fortune And Travel Absolutely Free!

by Ben and Nancy Dominitz

Have you heard about the fat commission checks and free travel benefits in the travel business? This book reveals how you can do both without losing a dime of your own money. Learn how to make money in your spare time and receive free travel and other discounts!
(6½ × 9½, 210 pp.) #1955; $20

$100,000 Phone Calls

by Mike Gilford

Could you use $200 an hour for just answering your phone? It can be yours for picking up the receiver and waiting for calls to come in. This is the most revolutionary money-making system you have ever heard of before. It is a business that allows you to take a 20% commission off work you never perform. The people that perform the work are more than willing to give you 20% because you will be offereing them more jobs than they will ever have time to do. This is a service that is badly needed. After you receive this book, you too can sit by the TV earning a 20% commission while others are out there doing the work for you. #4933; $10

$20,000 In 24 Hours And 130 Other Money-Making Reports

Did you ever wonder what companies give you when they offer to make you an instant millionaire overnight? Now, for the first time, almost every money-making plan and idea on the market has been compiled into one package.
(5½ × 8½,) #0333; $10

999 Little-Known Businesses That Can Make You A Fortune

by William Carruthers

This book is a collection of 999 businesses that have made their owners rich; these businesses can make you rich too. The majority of ideas require little or no capital and can be started in your spare time. It gives you such a large variety of projects to undertake that you are sure to find that perfect money-maker for you.
(5 × 8, 258 pp.) #2155; $10

How To Get Rich In Multi-Level Marketing

by David Holmes and Joel Andrews

You can get rich without working by using the multi-level approach. Your agents get the product from the company, but you get the commission from your agents and each agent they enlist. Others do the work while you sit back and collect the high commission.
(6 × 9, 114 pp.) #1855; $14.95

How To Use Your Hidden Potential To Get Rich

by David Bendah

Here's the path self-made millionaires took to make their fortunes, and now you too can follow this road to riches. No matter your skill, intelligence or experience, David Bendah shows you how to make your personal and financial dreams come true.
(6 × 9, 200 pp.) #0433; $12

$10,000 A Month Making PVC Furniture

by Sam Glassman

There is big money to be made in PVC Furniture. This book includes all the easy-to-follow plans, step-by-step instructions and a complete marketing plan that will show you how to sell your furniture to anxious buyers.
(6 x 9, 80 pp.) #2933; $7

The Complete Guide To Getting Free Grants And Low Interest Loans

by Lloyd Sanders

Three billion dollars are given away every year. Imagine being given hundreds of thousands of dollars just for the asking. Checks are mailed to your door because you mailed out a few letters. The amazing issuance system is also covered in the book. It is not a method of getting a loan, it is practically a handout. It is the best way possible to raise huge amounts of money very quickly! One man in New York who was $250,000 in debt, used this method to earn him $3.3 million in a few months. How is that for quick money?
#0633; $12

$15,000 For "Free Shopping"

by Brad Nolin

Imagine taking home $15,000 each time you go shopping. That's right, $15,000 for simple shopping that won't cost you a red cent. One man who lives in California became a multi-millionaire overnight, using this exact system. He now takes home $3,000,000 a year. Could you use $15,000 for doing simple shopping? Brad Nolin reveals his incredible method for making this dream a reality. A whole new life of wealth can be awaiting you. #4833; $10

$2,000 An Hour

by David Bendah

Would you like to stake your share of the $25 billion the government holds for you just by making a few phone calls and looking in some phone books? If you can read English and speak on the phone, you are on your way to making thousands of dollars overnight. This book shows you how you can make big money helping other people get their money from the government.
#0733; $12.95

ORDER BLANK — BEST SELLERS

- ☐ **The Ultimate Method of Making Instant Cash (#6633)** . . . . .Bob Kelly $12
- ☐ **$100,000 Refunds From the U.S. (#5422)** . . . . .William Kerth $15
- ☐ **Take My Free, Unique Packages (#1335)** . . . . .David Bendah $12
- ☐ **The Amazing Method of Reading People (#0533)** . . . . .Tom Foster $10
- ☐ **The $25 Billion Treasure (#3633)** . . . . .David Bendah $25
- ☐ **Building Your Million Dollar Empire (#5133)** . . . . .Mike Gilford $10
- ☐ **Grey Market Riches (#1733)** . . . . .Dan Webster $19.95
- ☐ **Instant Debt Relief, $100,000 Overnight! (3-book series) (#9933)** $29.95
- ☐ **$1,000,000 CashVision (#2744)** . . . . .Jeff Peters $12.95
- ☐ **$4,000 A Day Giving Away Special Books (#1336)** . . . . .Pete Branin $12
- ☐ **Billion Dollar Modeling Industry (#1033)** . . . . .Jeff Peters $12.95
- ☐ **Making $500,000 A Year In Mail Order (#1233)** . . . . .David Bendah $15
- ☐ **Winning at the Horse Races (#1933)** . . . . .Paul Lawrence $19.95
- ☐ **The Self Publisher's Opportunity Kit**
  (Kit includes 8 re-printable books) (#1633) $30
- ☐ **Cashing In on Government Money (#5033)** .Bill Kerth $12.95
- ☐ **Thousands of Dollars a Day With Your Camera (#2733)** . . . . .Jeff Peters $12.95
- ☐ **Poor Man's Way to Riches, Vol 1 (#3033)** . . . . .David Buckley $10
- ☐ **Poor Man's Way to Riches, Vol. 2 (#3133)** .David Buckley $10
- ☐ **Poor Man's Way to Riches, Vol. 3 (#3233)** .David Buckley $10
- ☐ **Poor Man's Way to Riches, Vol. 4 (#3333)** .David Buckley $10
- ☐ **Home Business Opportunities (#0877)** . . . . .Russ von Hoelscher $15
- ☐ **Cashing In on Government Surplus (#0938)** . . . . .Edward Kelly $14.95
- ☐ **Getting $100,000 of Free Advertising (#4053)** . . . . .George Strong $15
- ☐ **Getting the Government to Pay for Your New Business (#4055)** . . .George Strong $15
- ☐ **Making TV and Radio Advertising Pay Off (#4052)** . . . . .George Strong $15
- ☐ **Buy Real Estate With Nothing Down (#3858)** . . . . .Phillip Wellington $15
- ☐ **Getting Real Estate Next to Nothing**
  with Bankruptcies and Auctions (#3860) . . . . .Phillip Wellington $15
- ☐ **Get Rich With Foreclosures (#3861)** . . . . .Phillip Wellington $15
- ☐ **Become a Real Estate Millionaire (#3862)** . . . . .Phillip Wellington $15
- ☐ **Capital Raising Digest (#9934)** . . . . .Joseph Wright $15
- ☐ **Get Out Of Debt Forever (#9935)** . . . . .Joseph Wright $15
- ☐ **The Secrets of Getting Free Money (#3740)** . . . . .Joseph Wright $15
- ☐ **How to Get Any Credit Card You Want,**
  Even If You Have Bad Credit (#9937) . . . . .Joseph Wright $15

☐ Let the U.S. Gov't Make Your
Fortune in Real Estate (#3859)............................Phillip Wellington $15

☐ Take Your Junk Mail to the Bank (#0637).......................Larry Miller $12

☐ How to Make a Fortune from Direct Mail (#4050)..............George Strong $15

☐ Making Money From Display and Classified Ads (#4051).........George Strong $15

☐ You Can Make Millions In the
Import/Export Market (#3729).........................Samuel P. Wood $29.95

☐ Stay Home and Make Money (#2656)....................Russ von Hoelscher $15

☐ $12,000 Guaranteed in Just 3 Minutes (#0636)..................Sam Pitts $12.95

☐ Making Millions from Free Products (#3730)..................George Strong $15

☐ How to Get Anything You Want Absolutely
Free or Next to Nothing (#4733)..........................Phil Williams $10

☐ Make a Fortune and Travel
Absolutely Free! (#1955).....................Ben and Nancy Dominitz $20

☐ $100,000 Phone Calls (#4933)............................Mike Gilford $10

☐ $200,000 in 24 Hours and 130 Other
Money-Making Reports (#0333)..................................$10

☐ 999 Little-Known Businesses
That Can Make You a Fortune (#2155)...................William Carruthers $10

☐ How to Get Rich in Multi-Level Marketing
(#1855)...............................David Holmes and Joel Andrews $14.95

☐ How to Use Your Hidden Potential to Get Rich (#0433).........David Bendah $12

☐ How to Write a Good Advertisement (#1455).................Victor Schwab $15

☐ $10,000 a Month Making PVC Furniture (#2933)...............Sam Glassman $7

☐ The Complete Guide to Getting Free Grants
and Low Interest Loans (#0633)..........................Lloyd Sanders $12

☐ $15,000 for Shopping (#4833)............................Brad Nolin $10

☐ $2,000 An Hour(#0733)................................David Bendah $12.95

SEND ORDER TO:
Lion Publishing Co.
2801 Camino del Rio South
San Diego, CA 92108

(619) 543-9800
Call To Order
For Rush Delivery

Please send the books which are checked (in boxes on pages above). Enclosed is
$ _____ (Check or Money Order). If ordering one book, add $2 postage and handling.
If ordering two or more books, please add $1 per book.

BOOKS TO BE SENT TO:

Name _____

Address _____

City/State/Zip _____